LOFT DESIGN

SOLUTIONS FOR CREATING A LIVABLE SPACE

GLOUCESTER MASSACHUSETTS

ROCKPORT PUBLISHERS

First published in the United States of America by
Rockport Publishers, Inc.
33 Commercial Street
Gloucester, Massachusetts 01930-5089
Telephone: (978) 282-9590
Fax: (978) 283-2742
www.rockpub.com

Library of Congress Cataloging-in-Publication Data
Stone, Katherine
    Loft design: solutions for creating a livable space / Katherine
Stone.
        p.   cm.
    ISBN 1-56496-981-9 (hardcover)
    1. Lofts—Decoration I. Title
NK2117.L63S76 2005
747.88314—dc21
                                        2005008853
                                                CIP

ISBN 1-56496-981-9
10 9 8 7 6 5 4 3 2 1

Cover Design: Rule 29
Design: Roycroft Design (www.roycroftdesign.com)
Cover Image: Paul Warchol/Resolution 4 Architecture

Printed in China

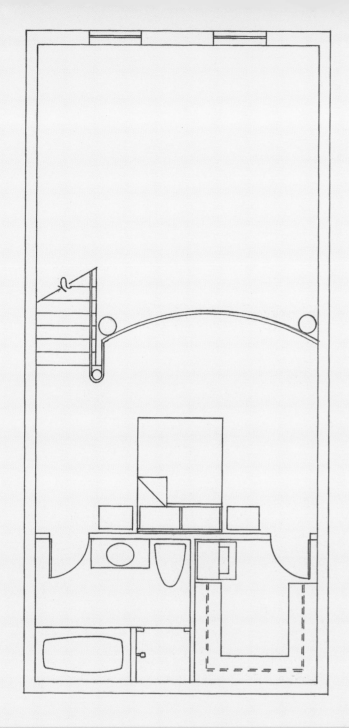

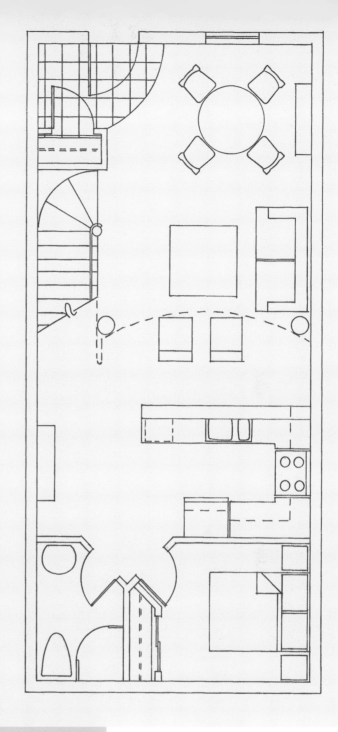

A Toronto loft sees the first step in the conversion process, the floor plan.

To my husband David and my son Bryan for their countless hours of aid and support.

Contents

✳ Introduction

In the early eighties, my husband and I set out to find a larger studio space for our design business. Everything I looked at was boring, mundane, and pedestrian. Then a photographer friend took me to look at his studio space.

We drove to a questionable part of town, parking in front of an abandoned wool mill that was more than 100 years old and sat on the banks of a river. The only inhabitants were the photographer, a strange guy who lived in the bowels of the building, and probably some rodents, which I chose not to think about. As we wandered through this piece of living history my mind raced, as any designer's would. Oh, the things I could do! Imagine it: three stories high, with an imposing tower at one end; a grand staircase and a gated freight elevator that linked each floor. There were no walls, just a colonnaded vista of open space and thousands of square feet. Remnants of the building's past life were intact—huge metal eyes screwed into the floor where machines had been bolted to; massive doors with a block-and-tackle weight system to slide them across tracks and enclose one wing; workers' initials carved into the towering support columns that dotted and segmented the cavernous void.

I chose a corner in close proximity to the elevator and stairs, where the imposing windows would give me the benefit of sunshine all day and a view of the city and water. I counted off the windows I wanted to define my studio and the first walls went up. Rejuvenating this neglected space signified a rebirth for this tired old lady. My husband and I brought the family to inspect our latest venture. Our children thought we were nuts. My mother-in-law recalled walking to the mill every day as a child to bring lunch in a pail to her mother, and that most of the workers had been women. They operated huge looms that wove wool into fabric for suiting.

Of our tenure there, I often reminisce about rollerblading in the still unclaimed areas; spiders setting off the burglar alarm so many times that the police refused to come anymore; working late and being terrified to venture outside my 2,000 square feet (186 square meters). I was so terrified that many times I slept over, and

eventually equipped the office with a sofa bed for that very purpose. I also mastered the art of releasing the elevator button at just the right moment so the floor of the elevator was in line with that of my destination. But most of all, I remember fantasizing about making this marvelous territory my home: I'd put the bathroom over there with a ceiling on it so the bedroom could go above; the kitchen would be open

to the living and dining areas; I'd put closets and storage against that perimeter wall; the kids could sleep beyond the low partition...

Circumstances changed and we moved again, but the concept grew. Today the building has been given some spit and polish, is full of thriving businesses, and each space has a generic name—a loft.

Chapter One

What Is a Loft?

Ask six people what a loft is and I bet you'll get six different answers. Even the dictionary isn't much help. According to Oxford, a loft is "an upper room covered by a house-roof, or a gallery in a church or hall." Webster's expands that definition to include "upper floors of a warehouse or business building, especially when not partitioned."

I had always thought of lofts as a mezzanine level overlooking an open space below, such as a hayloft in a barn. Since my involvement in the television series *Lofty Ideas*, my definition has expanded to include industrial space converted to residential living, even if nothing is done to change the appearance of the area except to throw a mattress on the floor for sleeping. So a water tower or a mechanic's garage converted to a home is a loft, just as a warehouse with the second floor overlooking the open, double-height living space is a loft.

What about new construction? Some cities are already running out of old industrial buildings to convert. From the developer's point of view, new construction is much cheaper and definitely easier. Imagine the problems inherent in trying to make an old warehouse like Pandora's box into a home with all the amenities people want, plus enough units to make the project financially feasible. So they've constructed new buildings with elements common to industrial lofts. Some are very good, and you generally have the advantage of being able to move right in, whereas unforeseen problems can often drag out the renovation of

an old building for years. However, the exteriors of newly constructed lofts are often disappointing because they're hard to distinguish from a typical high rise; and entering a low-ceiling foyer with a bank of elevators facing you certainly doesn't conjure up the image of an old warehouse. However, once you're inside the units, you can definitely create the feel of a loft.

The best compromise I've seen between new and old construction was of the "Oriental Warehouse" in San Francisco. The original building had deteriorated beyond the point of salvation, so the developer structurally shored up the exterior façade and then tore down the interior of the building itself. A new building was constructed inside, incorporating principles we all equate with lofts—spaciousness, large windows, open mezzanines, natural and industrial materials. When completed, it still looked like a derelict warehouse on the outside, but inside the owners enjoyed courtyards and balconies looking out through the original warehouse windows. It was very impressive.

< The "Oriental Warehouse" in San Francisco is a masterful example of historic preservation and urban renewal; from the curb it looks like an abandoned warehouse.

> The original façade of the "Oriental Warehouse" masks a structurally sound, state-of-the-art loft building built within its perimeter.

So What's the Big Deal?

Just as any real estate agent will tell you, first on my short list of why lofts are so appealing is *location, location, location!*

By necessity, industrial buildings built prior to the turn of the twentieth century were located near water, which was the most common means of transport. Cities developed and grew around industry, and therefore around industrial buildings. However, when technology and cheap labor provided by developing countries made these buildings redundant, they were abandoned, causing city cores to deteriorate and become hotbeds for crime.

Artists opened our eyes to the possibility of alternative living. Attracted by cheap rent and enormous open spaces in which to create their masterpieces on a grand scale, they moved in. Their occupation of these spaces was often illegal, as most were zoned industrial or commercial. The buildings weren't equipped with the requisite sprinklers and fire escapes that today's residential occupancy codes call for. This type of illegal living is not a thing of the past either. Many of these old buildings, prior to being reclaimed (hopefully, as opposed to being torn down) are discreetly home to the artists who work in them.

Baby boomers watched this bohemian lifestyle with envy until, as empty nesters, they opted to take a walk on the wild side and abandon their manicured, picket-fenced suburban homes for the concrete laden, low-maintenance city life. The appeal of **unimpeded space** as opposed

< *This home is a perfect example of a typical loft in a newly constructed building. On entering, we're confronted with a living room that's hard to distinguish from a standard condominium. While the ceilings have been left concrete, the critical element of volume is missing when you enter.*

to boxy rooms is hard to resist; throw in a waterfront view and it's impossible. Gen-Xers appear to have grown up with the urban lifestyle in their blood and were drawn immediately to life in the crowded city center with virtually everything (except the country!) at their fingertips.

Size is also a big attraction. Remember these buildings were constructed to house large-scale machinery. They were also built prior to the use of electricity, making huge windows a necessity to maximize the length of the workday. There aren't too many downtown condominiums that can boast about 17-foot (5.2 meter) high ceilings with 9-foot (2.7 meter) windows, but that's pretty average in a loft.

Last on my appeal shortlist is **open space**. Lofts are usually sold raw, which means with no interior walls in place. This necessitates examination of how you, as an individual, live. Most of us wouldn't stop to think about this. We're used to fashioning how we live based on a developer's ideal. But often their decisions on space planning are based as much on economics as ease of living.

I can't tell you what a sense of freedom and satisfaction this planning process brings to people. It can be a painful decision-making ordeal but the results are liberating. When the construction dust settles, what's left is a space totally **customized** to how you want to live. The same result is achieved when you design and build a custom home, except with a loft there's no grass to cut.

> *It's not until we reach the back of the home that we get the impression of a true loft: the two-storied dining room with the window walls, the soaring concrete column, and the bedroom overlook on the opposite side create a sense of openness and space associated with lofts.*

> ⌄ The first step on the road to conversion is to identify your needs and then articulate them into a workable floor plan.

> ‹ The prospect of transforming a raw cavity into a home can intimidate the heartiest of souls.

FURNITURE PLAN
SCALE 1/4"=1'-0"

Getting Started

You've taken the leap and are now the proud owner of a loft—the trouble is it bears no resemblance to a home. The question I'm always presented with is **"Where do I start?"** In most cases the developer of the building will be able to offer advice, suggest layouts for the space, or provide a complete finished product. The latter is usually the most cost-effective solution if you're purchasing the space as a complete package for a fixed price on a budget. Professionals can save you time and money, believe it or not, by focusing on your project and knowing exactly where to get the perfect products so you achieve the biggest bang for your buck. They can relieve you of the tedium of overseeing and managing your renovation. While exercising their expertise, you can be making money at what you do best, something often overlooked.

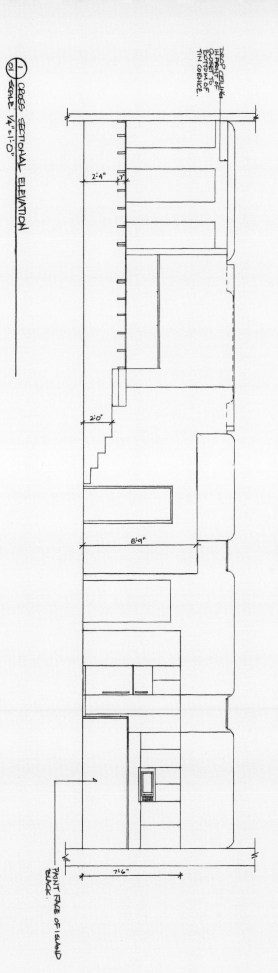

CROSS SECTIONAL ELEVATION
SCALE 1/4" = 1'-0"

DROP CEILING
IN FRONT OF
CLOSET TO
BOTTOM OF
TIN CORNICE.

2'-4"

2'-0"

8'-9"

7'-6"

PAINT FACE OF ISLAND
BLACK.

> An elevation of the floor plan allows you to see the relationship between the floors, walls, and ceilings.

Hiring Professionals

An **architect or interior designer** can help you realize your dream. What's the difference between the two? Not much when you're dealing with interior space. Professional interior designers are educated in interior construction and will be up-to-date with elements pertaining to living spaces, such as layouts, lighting, finishes, and fixtures. After all, that's their business. They can establish and instigate a vision for your loft from raw space to window dressings.

Use professionals who are registered with government approved associations to ensure an established standard of education, experience, and competence, as well as adherence to professional standards, and a requirement for liability insurance. Look for letters such as ASID (American Society of Interior Designers) or RAIC (The Royal Architectural Institute of Canada). Choose the services of someone who has the qualifications needed for your project, whether you're dividing up the space or putting up window dressings.

Ask around for recommendations from people whose spaces you admire and you know had help achieving that look. Word of mouth is a good thermometer. Ask friends if the architect or designer was congenial to work with, if he or she stayed within the budget confines, if the work progressed at a steady pace. And most importantly, ask if they are happy with the end result. I liken construction to childbirth—it can be the worst pain you think you'll ever endure, but as soon as it's over it's forgotten because of what you have gained.

< (far left) It's exhilarating to watch
the progression from raw area to
paper dreams to a concrete entity.

< (left) Once the paintbrushes
come out, you're almost there.
The finishing touches are the
hardest to bear; setting up home
finally feels like a reality.

Dare to Compare

When you've got some names, look at samples of their completed work.
Do you like their style? **Compare fees.** Professional architects and
designers can base their fees on a percentage of the overall cost of the
work, a flat fee determined by the scope, or a billing system similar to a
lawyers where they charge an hourly rate plus expenses. Typical hourly
fees can range from $60 to $200 per hour to no fee if you purchase all
your building materials and products from them. I'd stay away from
that one. You might find yourself being shown only products that have
a large profit margin, or only items that they represent.

In my design practice, we charge either a flat fee or a hourly rate on
small projects, and a percentage on the work prescribed for extensive
projects. We supply our clients with products of their choosing at a
discounted price (wholesale plus a small handling fee to cover the time
spent by the purchasing department for procurement). Buying through
a design firm can actually offset the designer's fee, and the world
becomes your department store. Finally, arrange to meet in person with
the people you're considering working with. You'll find that it's a closer
relationship than the one you share with your doctor or lawyer, so it's
important to have compatible personalities.

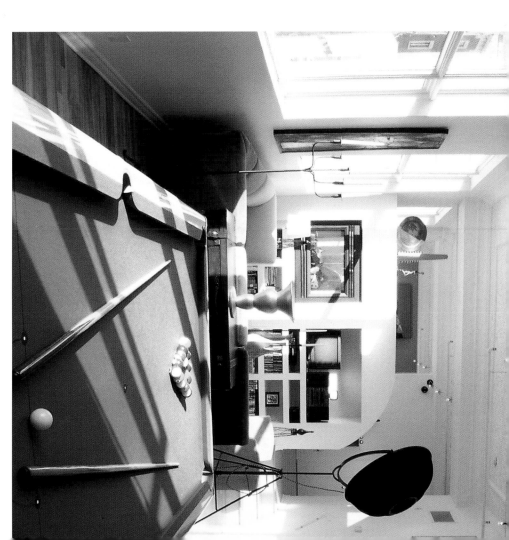

^ With the ceiling expanse exposed,
a small space appears much more
spacious. The bedroom and guest
bedroom cum laundry room, hall,
and home office all receive their
modicum of privacy by changing
floor levels and installing partitions
that float below the ceiling.

When you've reached a decision, **decide on a budget** for what you want to accomplish, and provide this in writing. Your hired help can then assess if you've allotted sufficient funds, and will have a figure to work toward. I think the most difficult aspect of being a designer is meeting the expectations of a client within their budget parameters. The relationship will be stronger if this is addressed immediately.

Designers and architects often offer consultation services and this is a great option if you're doing the work yourself. You can bring in professionals, paid on an hourly basis, at the critical stages, such as at the beginning of the planning stage to pick their brain for possible layout ideas or to bounce your preliminary concepts off them. Set up another meeting for your final plan. They can help with color, furniture selections, plumbing fixtures—just about everything.

The Self-Sufficient Loft Owner

The other option on the road from industrial space to a home is to forge ahead yourself. This is not as far-fetched as it may sound. If you are brave, have a confident sense of design, and know some talented tradespeople (carpenters, plumbers, electricians) to whom you can accurately express your loft objectives, the results can be a very personal and successful statement. And you'll have the added bonus of taking pride in your work and accepting the accolades.

Evaluate and assess what you want your space to accomplish. Refer to magazines, books, movies, and television shows, such as *Lofty Ideas*, for the look you want to achieve. Read books like this one to facilitate an understanding of the process and to determine the limitations that you may have to deal with. Then blaze a trail into the world of design.

< *The sleek interior of an "Oriental Warehouse" loft basks in the natural light transmitted through the original factory window openings in the brick wall beyond. The double height windows installed on the face of the interior building are shared on the two levels of the loft.*

Chapter Two

Space Planning

Capturing the essence of a loft is dependant on how you lay out the space. Don't confuse this with the style—that comes later. Start with a basic floor plan of the area you're dealing with. There are a number of ways you can accomplish this. Look in your yellow pages under "drafting" or "home plans." The listed companies will come to your loft, accurately measure the space, and then draw it to scale, leaving you with a plan on which to plot your dream.

You can also purchase drafting paper, measure, and create your own drawing. If you are adept at the computer, there are several programs on the market that are user-friendly; and a digital plan can be easily modified. From your base plan, you can add walls, and then furniture, without having to constantly copy the plan. Either way, remember to include any unique characteristics that you want to add or that you want to retain. A signature feature of these industrial buildings are the columns that were evenly spaced for support. These are functional, and if you plan on removing them, you'll have to install an alternative support mechanism. This will involve an engineer to ensure the stability of the roof so your neighbors above don't land on top of you!

A **plan** is scaled to size, like a map. Have it drawn in the simplest measurement you understand, such as ¼ inch equals 1 foot (1:50 in metric). Scaled furniture templates are available in these dimensions, so if you're going to develop your own furniture plan, make it compatible.

Planning Tips

1 Prepare a scaled drawing of your space.

2 Assess what you need.

3 List what you want.

4 Familiarize yourself with your local building code.

‹ The objective of loft planning is to create intimate areas within an open space. Opaque glass doors admit natural light while sliding on ceiling tracks for maximum flexibility and exposed volume.

Basic Measurement of Length, Conversions, Symbols, and Abbreviations for ARCHITECTURAL DRAWINGS

BASICS	EXAMPLE
Standard lowercase type is used for unit names and symbols	10 square feet, or 10 sq ft
Unit names are used in the plural for values greater than 1, equal to 0, or less than -1	1 meter, 10 meters, 0 meters
A space is left between the unit name of symbol and a number	10 feet
In North America, the decimal point is a dot placed on the line	.01
Elsewhere the decimal point can be denoted by a comma or a raised dot	,01 or ·01

SCALES	
1" = 1'0" (25.4 mm = 304.8 mm)	1:10
1/2" = 1'0" (12.7 mm = 304.8 mm)	1:20
1/4" = 1'0" (6.35 mm = 304.8 mm) This is the favored scale for floor plans	1:50
1/8" = 1'0" (3 mm = 304.8 mm)	1:100

ABBREVIATIONS	
Width	w
Length	l
Depth	d
Height	h
Square	sq.
"By"	x
Plans in imperial measurement are always expressed as feet and inches	1'0"
Metric plans at 1:50 and 1:100 are expressed in millimeters	304.8 mm

Measurements Used on Plans

UNIT	PLURAL	SYMBOL	METRIC EQUIVALENT	PLURAL	SHORT FORM	CONVERSION
Inch	Inches	"	Millimeter	Millimeters	mm	1 inch = 25.4 mm
Foot	Feet	' or ft	Meter	Meters	m	1 foot = 0.3048 meters
Square Foot	Square Feet	ft² or sq ft	Square Meter	Square Meters	m²	1 square foot = 0.092903 m²

The overall area of a space is expressed in square feet or square meters by multiplying the length by the width. Length from the back of the space to the front is 30'0", the width between the two side walls is 12'0" therefore the area is 30'0" x 12'0" = 360 sq. ft. In metric it would be 9.14 m x 3.66 m = 33.45 m².

> You can read the plan with a regular ruler by lining it up on the inside of the window wall. It will measure 6 1/4 inches (159 mm), but because this is in 1/4 inch (1:50; 1 mm on the drawing equals 50 real mm) scale, meaning every 1/4 of an inch (6 mm) is equal to 1 foot (.3 meter), 6 1/4 inches (159 mm) is in fact 25 quarters, therefore the wall is 25 feet (7.6 m) long. You can also purchase a triangular shaped "scale" ruler in either metric or imperial measure, from an art supply store. Each side of the ruler depicts a different scale measurement. If you lay the 1/4 inch (6 mm) side down on the same window wall it will read 25, which translates to 25 feet (7.6 meters).

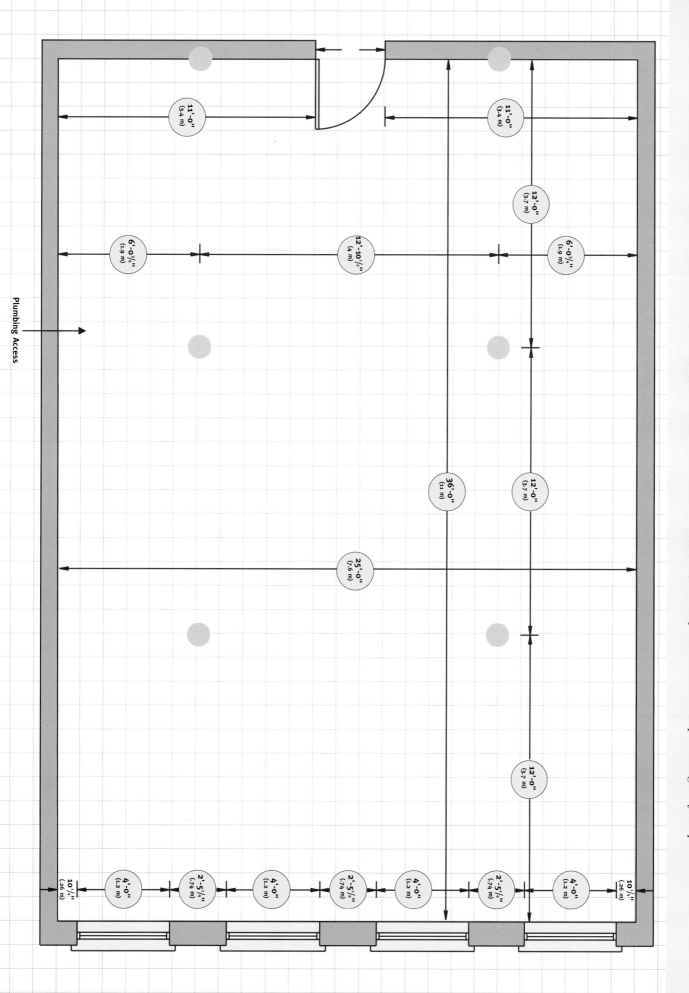

How to Build a Plan

Include the location of windows, the access to your loft, structural details such as columns, and any services such as plumbing on your plan.

Plumbing Access

11'-0" (3.4 m)
11'-0" (3.4 m)
12'-0" (3.7 m)
6'-0¾" (1.9 m)
12'-10½" (4 m)
6'-0¾" (1.9 m)
36'-0" (11 m)
12'-0" (3.7 m)
25'-0" (7.6 m)
12'-0" (3.7 m)
10¼" (.26 m)
4'-0" (1.2 m)
2'-5¼" (.74 m)
4'-0" (1.2 m)
2'-5½" (.74 m)
4'-0" (1.2 m)
2'-5¼" (.74 m)
4'-0" (1.2 m)
10¼" (.26 m)

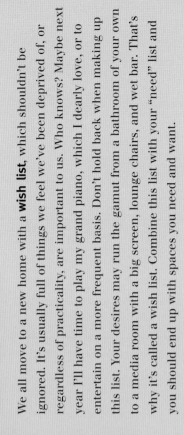

What Do I Want?

We all move to a new home with a **wish list**, which shouldn't be ignored. It's usually full of things we feel we've been deprived of, or regardless of practicality, are important to us. Who knows? Maybe next year I'll have time to play my grand piano, which I dearly love, or to entertain on a more frequent basis. Don't hold back when making up this list. Your desires may run the gamut from a bathroom of your own to a media room with a big screen, lounge chairs, and wet bar. That's why it's called a wish list. Combine this list with your "need" list and you should end up with spaces you need and want.

< (far left) Classic lanterns suspended over the living area visually reduce the ceiling height to a more comfortable level for conversation.

< (left) A long corridor is broken up with recessed doorways and focal points to make the journey enjoyable—an oversize painting, a floor sculpture replacing the cables that used to occupy the recess, and a beckoning window signifying the terminus.

What Do I Need?

Figuring out how to divide your **space** and what **functions** need to be incorporated is the difficult part. Start with what you need. Have your day planner or calendar for the past year handy.

Write down the rooms you used in the past day, week, month, four-month period, and year. If you're currently living in a small space where functions are doubled up in areas, list the functions instead. Write in any additional rooms or functions not listed.

< Design traits abound in this loft: angling the furniture settings adds an edge to the static space, the grid pattern of the windows is repeated on the carpeting, and accessories and furnishings of varying height separate groupings while drawing the eye up.

What Do I Want?   *for me*

- ✔ A dining room/ table (for how many?)   6-26 people
- ✔ A guest bedroom   times 2
- ✔ A home office
- ☐ An area for formal entertaining
- ✔ A TV room (family room)
- ☐ An eat-in kitchen
- ☐ A chef's kitchen
- ✔ A utilitarian kitchen
- ✔ An area to workout
- ✔ A personal bathroom
- ✔ A powder room
- ✔ A second bathroom for guests
- ✔ An outside space
- ✔ A grand piano
- _____
- _____
- _____
- _____
- _____

What Do You Want?   *for you*

- ☐ A dining room/table (for how many?)
- ☐ A guest bedroom
- ☐ A home office
- ☐ An area for formal entertaining (living room)
- ☐ A TV room (family room)
- ☐ An eat-in kitchen
- ☐ A chef's kitchen
- ☐ A utilitarian kitchen
- ☐ An area to workout
- ☐ A personal bathroom
- ☐ A powder room
- ☐ A second bathroom for guests
- ☐ An outside space
- ☐ _____
- ☐ _____
- ☐ _____
- ☐ _____
- ☐ _____

How Much Space?

The following chart lists average sizes for common rooms. To determine the **square footage** of a space, multiply the length by the width. Adding up my square footages, I should be looking for a loft of at least 1,500 square feet (139 square meters) with an allowance for passageways of 4 feet (1.2 meters) wide by 40 feet (12.2 meters) long. However, like most people, I've already bought my loft and it's an average size—900 square feet (84 square meters) or 25 feet (7.6 meters) wide by 36 feet (11.0 meters) long—a typical long, narrow format.

‹ Lofts have liberated kitchens and placed them front and center without imposing boundary walls. The cook can share in the action of the entire environment.

˄ The exposed steel trusses of this open air loft help to define the area below while reducing the vast ceiling height.

Average Space of Common Rooms

ROOM AND FUNCTIONS	AREA REQUIRED	
Small Entrance	4' x 4' (1.2 m x 1.2 m)	16 sq ft (1.5 m²)
Grand Entrance	12' x 12' (3.7 m x 3.7 m)	144 sq ft (13 m²)
Parallel Wall Kitchen	6' x 12' (1.8 m x 3.7 m)	72 sq ft (6.7 m²)
U-Shaped Kitchen	8' x 12' (2.4 m x 3.7 m)	96 sq ft (8.9 m²)
Living Room	12' x 15' (3.7 m x 4.6 m)	180 sq ft (16.7 m²)
Grand Piano	5' x 7' (1.5 m x 2.1 m)	35 sq ft (3.3 m²)
Dining Room	9' x 12' (2.7 m x 3.7 m)	108 sq ft (10 m²)
Per Person Dining Area	2' x 3'5" (.61 m x 1.1 m)	7 sq ft (.7 m²)
Family Room	12' x 15' (3.7 m x 4.6 m)	180 sq ft (16.7 m²)
Big Screen Television	3' x 4' (.9 m x 1.2 m)	12 sq ft (1.1 m²)
King Bedroom (walk-in closets)	13' x 16' (4 m x 4.9 m)	192 sq ft (17.8 m²)
King Bedroom (wall closets)	13' x 13' (4 m x 4 m)	169 sq ft (15.7 m²)
Bathroom with Whirlpool Tub	8' x 12' (2.4 m x 3.7 m)	96 sq ft (8.9 m²)
Exercise Area	7' x 7' (2.1 m x 2.1 m)	49 sq ft (4.6 m²)
Queen Bedroom	10' x 12' (3 m x 3.7 m)	120 sq ft (11.1 m²)
Four Piece Bath	8' x 7' (2.4 m x 2.1 m)	56 sq ft (5.2 m²)
Three Piece Bath	5' x 7' (1.5 m x 2.1 m)	35 sq ft (3.2 m²)
Powder Room	3' x 8' (.9 m x 2.4 m)	24 sq ft (2.2 m²)
Computer Work Station	5' x 6' (1.5 m x 1.8 m)	30 sq ft (2.8 m²)
Billiard Table (4' x 8' [1.22 m x 2.4 m])	12' x 16' (3.7 m x 4.9 m)	192 sq ft (17.8 m²)
Storage Closet	5' x 6' (1.5 m x 1.8 m)	30 sq ft (2.8 m²)
Outdoor Space	6' x 12' (1.5 m x 3.7 m)	72 sq ft (6.7 m²)

Block It Out, Baby!

A block plan is developed from your list. Each area is "blocked" onto the **floor plan**. The block lines do not indicate walls or how you get in and out of rooms. It's only allotment for functions. I usually start at the window wall and work back placing areas that are the most important to me first.

> The block plan is designed to give you a general overview without too much initial effort. It should help you define your priorities and aid in the process of elimination. Check out the rooms spilling out of my loft!

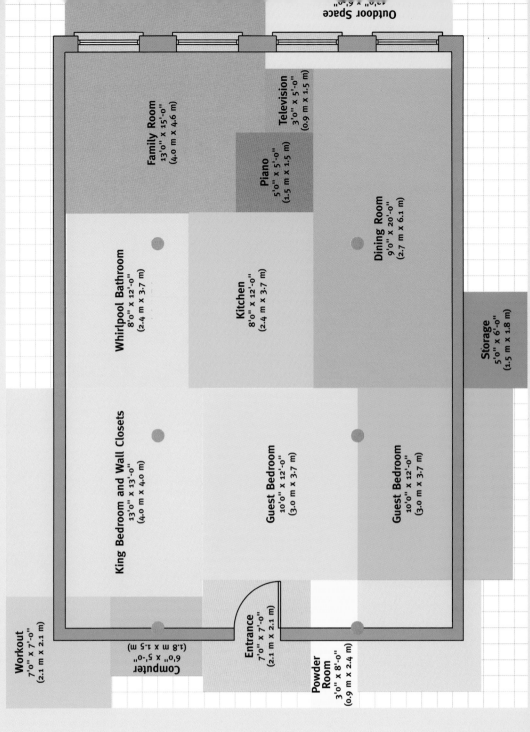

Workout
7'0" x 7'-0"
(2.1 m x 2.1 m)

Computer
6'0" x 5'-0"
(1.8 m x 1.5 m)

Entrance
7'0" x 7'-0"
(2.1 m x 2.1 m)

Powder Room
3'0" x 8'-0"
(0.9 m x 2.4 m)

King Bedroom and Wall Closets
13'0" x 13'-0"
(4.0 m x 4.0 m)

Whirlpool Bathroom
8'0." x 12'-0"
(2.4 m x 3.7 m)

Family Room
13'0" x 15'-0"
(4.0 m x 4.6 m)

Guest Bedroom
10'0" x 12'-0"
(3.0 m x 3.7 m)

Kitchen
8'0" x 12'-0"
(2.4 m x 3.7 m)

Piano
5'0." x 5'-0"
(1.5 m x 1.5 m)

Television
3'0" x 5'-0"
(0.9 m x 1.5 m)

Guest Bedroom
10'0" x 12'-0"
(3.0 m x 3.7 m)

Dining Room
9'0" x 20'-0"
(2.7 m x 6.1 m)

Storage
5'0" x 6'-0"
(1.5 m x 1.8 m)

Outdoor Space

Time for a Reality Check

The block plan is an uncluttered visual representation of **proportions** and what I see is an inordinate amount devoted to minimal use—the guest bathroom and bedroom. Acknowledging this, in the next stage I'll work to make them more compact.

Reality will set in when your block plan is complete. You may be lucky enough to have more space than you need, but more likely it will indicate the need to compromise. This means doubling up on functions, which isn't necessarily a bad thing. Look at areas that could be dual purpose, such as a guest room/home office combination; the pool table that converts to a dining table for twenty; or a powder room that also has a shower for overnight guests.

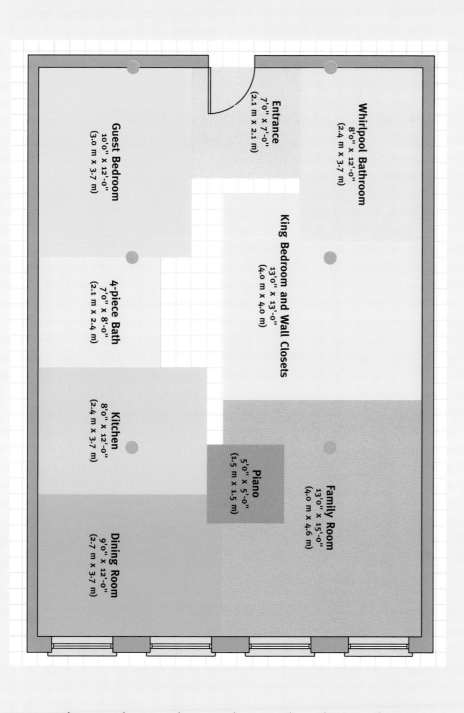

Whirlpool Bathroom
8'0" x 12'-0"
(2.4 m x 3.7 m)

Entrance
7'0" x 7'-0"
(2.1 m x 2.1 m)

King Bedroom and Wall Closets
13'0" x 13'-0"
(4.0 m x 4.0 m)

Guest Bedroom
10'0" x 12'-0"
(3.0 m x 3.7 m)

4-piece Bath
7'0" x 8'-0"
(2.1 m x 2.4 m)

Kitchen
8'0" x 12'-0"
(2.4 m x 3.7 m)

Piano
5'0" x 5'-0"
(1.5 m x 1.5 m)

Family Room
13'0" x 15'-0"
(4.0 m x 4.6 m)

Dining Room
9'0" x 12'-0"
(2.7 m x 3.7 m)

My compromises:

◆ **Workout** in bedroom or living room

◆ Put **computer** in guest bedroom

◆ Replace the powder room with a four-piece **guest bathroom**

◆ Utilize closets in the guest bedrooms for **storage**

◆ Go to the movies instead of watching a **big screen television**

◆ Allow for the **dining table** to expand into the living room

◆ Send one couple to a hotel

Can You Double Up?

If your loft has a very high ceiling, you may be willing to sacrifice some of this height to a mezzanine that overlooks the living area, or a second floor complete with individual rooms. Rooms that benefit from the intimacy of lower ceilings are kitchens, bathrooms, bedrooms, and dining rooms; or use the rooms as storage, on a utilitarian note.

Local **building codes** vary on the minimum height requirements for adding living space above, so check with your municipal building department. I would consider anything less than 7 feet (2.1 meters) questionable for comfort. Individual taste reigns supreme here, even though some may contravene codes. I've seen loft bedrooms where you crawled from the top of the stairs onto the bed, and the ceiling was only inches from your face. I couldn't sleep there.

There are also some **space-saving innovations** that have been accepted as structurally sound alternatives to the standard floor construction method. A typical floor assembly averages around 13 inches (330 mm) but many local codes are accepting 2-inch (51 mm) thick Douglas fir boards as the structural material, and it can double as the ceiling below. The inches saved can be critical to the feasibility of upper levels.

‹ Look for impact in your placement of a mezzanine so the height differences are accentuated. By placing the tiered rooms to the side or by the entrance, the double height will explode in front of you.

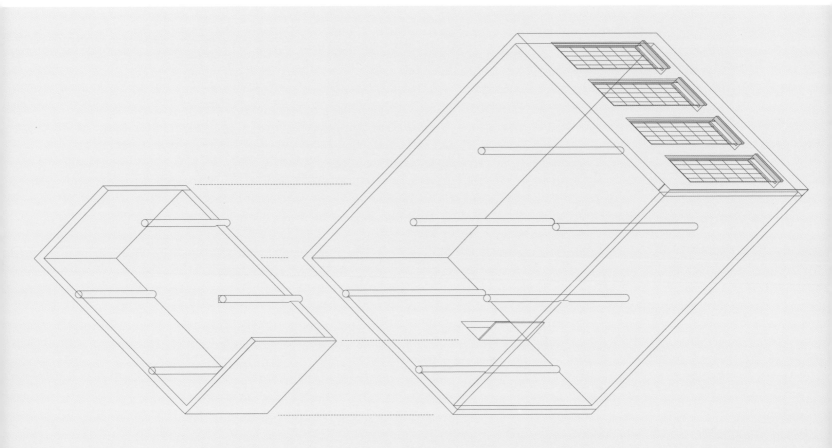

But I Want It All!

For those in the enviable position of having **excess space**, consider expropriating some interior square footage and devoting it to exterior usage. We often hear the old adage "you can't have everything," but I believe, like the Rolling Stones, that with careful planning, you can "get what you need." One of the biggest drawbacks with loft living is the lack of access to the outdoors. Regardless of sound, smog, and other pollutants of city life, it's still nice to have a personal and private area where you can enjoy a cup of coffee and the newspaper on a sunny Sunday morning or where you can cultivate a container garden.

There are several ways of attaining an airy retreat, some more invasive or expensive than others, but none particularly difficult to achieve. A new exterior wall can be constructed inside the present parameters, replicating window placement with the inclusion of an access door in one of the openings; new walls can be finished to match the existing ones or clad in an appropriate contrasting material. Alternatively, a curtain wall of glass doors will heighten the quality of translucency within and obscure the division between interior and exterior landscapes.

Another option is to incorporate architecturally pleasing reclaimed doors, adding a design element to the premises.

When planning an outdoor space, be sure to consider your neighbors below—treat the floor like a shower base and make it waterproof, complete with a drain to safely remove excess water. The ceiling will also have to be changed—interior drywall will not withstand outdoor conditions. Remove any drywall and replace it with an exterior material such as concrete, wood siding, or aluminum. Depending on the climate of your area, the newly acquired terrace can be treated as an extension of your loft, complete with a ceiling fan, fireplace, ceramic tile floor, and requisite furnishings.

Finally, take the time to consider when you would be most likely to enjoy the outdoors—in the morning for coffee, or in the evening for dinners accompanied by the setting sun? Take note of the streetscape; is one side of the building quieter than the other side? These factors will all come into play when positioning your outdoor haven.

< *Carve out a terrace by constructing new exterior walls within the loft and removing the glazing from the original window openings.*

^ When you open up a central portion of your loft to the elements, you are doubly blessed with an enclosed retreat that is protected from wind and noise.

An **inner courtyard** open to the sky is another possibility for incorporating an outdoor space, allowing the penetration of natural light to the central core of the loft where direct sunlight is scarce. Obviously this will only work if you happen to be on the top floor, unless the vista you want to penetrate is your neighbor's living room! If you own the building, it's a great way to bring light into more units than may be physically possible from the original design of the structure. Industrial workplaces were never designed to capture the view; that would have been too distracting to the workers. However, local codes require that residential occupancies have some penetration of natural light, so an open courtyard or a glazed atrium could solve this technical problem.

The least invasive ways to attain **fresh air** access are via French doors protected with a rail guard, or a Juliet balcony that extends just beyond the face of the building. French doors open into the loft and a series of them would definitely add an **alfresco** feeling on a sunny day. You'll need to consider how the addition of new windows will impact the appearance of the structure and then present your case to the building owner for permission.

Rooftops are generally undeveloped territory waiting for reclamation. Ensure the stability of the roof and the support system below before embarking on your transformation. It can be as simple as rolling out some artificial turf and plopping a lawn chair down or as complex as a built-up roof system that will allow you to create a veritable oasis in a concrete urban landscape. The bubbling of a water feature or the rustle of ornamental grasses can mask street noise. You will be creating a personal sanctuary and the addition of plantings will improve the quality of the air you breathe.

> *The breathtaking view rounds out this ultimate rooftop conversion complete with pergola, fountain and manicured shrubs.*

^ Straight-run stairs, as the name implies, have no turns. They are the least expensive and most practical in terms of design styles.

< On your plans, the stairs will look like this.

Step It Out

The **stairs** required for access to a roof or mezzanine can extradite considerable living space—well worth it in my opinion—but it's another thing to be considered in the plan. Think carefully about the placement; open stairs can enhance a loft of grand scale and casually define an amorphous floor plan; or they can take a less prominent position running up a perimeter wall.

> "L" stairs have a landing at some point in the run that changes the direction of the stairs at a 90-degree angle. Where space is at a premium, pie-shaped stairs called winders can replace the landing. Winders can be dangerous as they narrow to several inches at the apex.

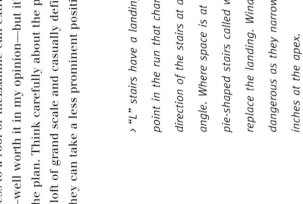

^ "U" stairs run parallel to each other at different planes connected by a landing.

How Many Steps Do I Need?

Below are some **calculations** that will give you a pretty close estimate of the area your stairs will occupy.

Calculate your rise by measuring the floor to ceiling height in your loft. Subtract one foot (.3 meters) from this dimension and divide by two. This will give you the ceiling height of the upper and lower level. The division of height is at your discretion and will ultimately be dependant upon the intended use of the space. Living comfort translates into seven feet (2.1 meters) or more while storage can be lower.

Stairways: Spatial Needs and Considerations

1. The most comfortable step height is around 7" (179 mm), so to determine the number of steps you're going to need divide 95½" (2,426 mm) by 7" (179 mm), which equals just over 15. You can therefore have 15 steps at 7.15" (186 mm) high each.

2. Stairs typically run at a slope between 30 and 35 degrees with a tread depth of between 10½" (267 mm) to 12" (305 mm). To calculate how much floor area your stairs will occupy, multiply the tread depth of 10½" (267 mm) by the number of steps, keeping in mind the floor of the second level serves as a step, so there is always one less tread than rise. The product of 10½" (267 mm) multiplied by 14 is 147" (3,734 mm). If the stairs are 42" (1,067 mm) wide they will take up an area 147" x 42" (3,734 mm x 1,067 mm) or 12' 3" x 3' 6" (3.68 m x 1.1 m). This isn't lost space. The space under the stairway can be left open so you can walk or display underneath, or it can be enclosed for storage.

3. In most loft scenarios, the stairs are placed below the double height ceiling, but if you start them under the mezzanine, remember to allow for headroom, usually 6' 8" (2.0 m) by code. This has to be open space above.

< Spiral stairs are the most compact but are also the most difficult to navigate on a regular basis. Because they are virtually impassable with furniture, make sure your king-size bed and whirlpool tub are hoisted through the opening before the stairs are in place.

The Letter of the Law

Building codes are rules and regulations pertaining to the construction of your home. They've been made in reaction to unfortunate events that have transpired, or could transpire, and are there for your safety. They aren't meant to be punitive or to cramp your style. Written sets of minimum standards are in place for each country, province, or state. In addition, local municipalities can contravene these codes, and enforce their own measures. It's a good idea to contact your local building department and become aware of the restrictions that apply. Most municipalities require that you present your plans to the building department before you start construction. They are scrutinized for compliance to the codes, and only when they do comply will the department issue a building permit. Find out what renovations require a permit—you may be surprised.

A building inspector must provide you with an occupancy permit before you're legally allowed to move into a renovated property. All those wonderful features we admire because of their "suspended in space" appearance, like open stair railings, are usually not legal. When asked how they got away with it, the most common response is that a temporary solution that conformed to the building code was installed until after the inspection and receipt of the occupancy papers. Mezzanines below allowable height were listed as storage spaces; stairs and railings were constructed inexpensively, or borrowed if they happened to fit the situation.

For your own protection, both from a safety and liability perspective, work at finding a design solution that creatively meets the minimum code requirements. Point in fact: Lifelong friends get together for a social evening. The guest becomes a little unsteady and falls under an improperly guarded mezzanine. He is now a quadriplegic in the process of suing his former friend. Two lives irreparably damaged for the sake of aesthetics. Makes a pretty poor case. So, please, follow the codes for your own well-being.

∧ Advances in technology have
made illusory effects and safety
simpatico as these architectural-cast
glass stair treads attest.

Achieving Your Ultimate Block Plan

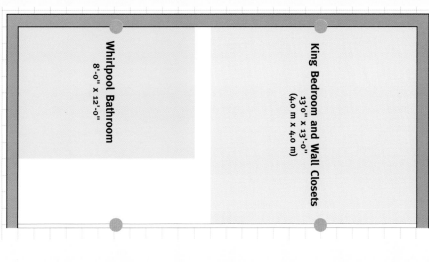

Second Floor

King Bedroom and Wall Closets
13'0" x 13'-0"
(4.0 m x 4.0 m)

Whirlpool Bathroom
8'-0" x 12'-0"

< *My "ultimate block plan" is achieved by adding a second floor for the master bedroom and private bath. This leaves room on the main floor for my grand piano and a terrace.*

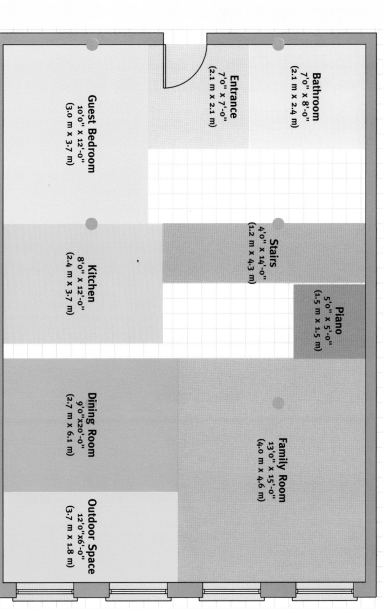

First Floor

Bathroom
7'-0" x 8'-0"
(2.1 m x 2.4 m)

Entrance
7'0" x 7'-0"
(2.1 m x 2.1 m)

Guest Bedroom
10'0" x 12'-0"
(3.0 m x 3.7 m)

Stairs
4'-0" x 14'-0"
(1.2 m x 4.3 m)

Piano
5'0" x 5'-0"
(1.5 m x 1.5 m)

Kitchen
8'-0" x 12'-0"
(2.4 m x 3.7 m)

Dining Room
9'0"x20'-0"
(2.7 m x 6.1 m)

Family Room
13'0" x 15'-0"
(4.0 m x 4.6 m)

Outdoor Space
12'0"x6'-0"
(3.7 m x 1.8 m)

Chapter Three

Room by Room

With the necessities blocked in, we can start on the floor plan. This will be the most time consuming and challenging part of the design process. Floor plans evolve from a general layout to a comprehensive plan as kitchens, baths, furniture, and walls define the area.

< Impressive factory doors are remnants of the building's past. A distinctive feature of the loft, they're worthy of designing the interior layout around.

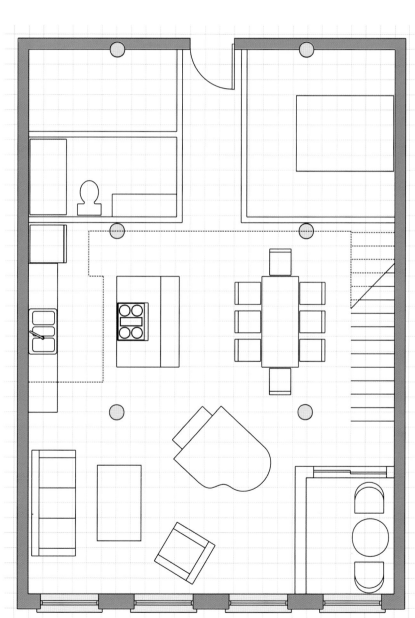

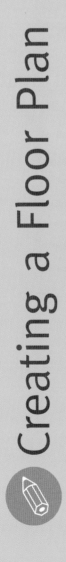

Creating a Floor Plan

< *Powder rooms are most appropriate when located near the entrance. However, if it's also doubling as a guest bathroom with a shower, position it between the living area and sleeping quarters.*

Here are some guidelines to keep in mind when laying out your space:

◆ **Even in the smallest loft, allow yourself an entrance foyer.** Don't just walk into the living room. This doesn't mean throwing up walls—a section of floor left open, a column, a closet, a change in floor material or a drop ceiling can all indicate a foyer. The space beyond the foyer should unfold before you.

◆ **If you're working on a budget,** try placing rooms requiring plumbing together in a horizontal line, in a pod, or stacked if you have a two-story loft. The rooms should also be close to the existing building plumbing; the shorter the pipes, the lower your plumbing bill.

◆ **Locate the bedroom in the quietest part of the loft.** Check for street noise. Try and avoid placing the master bedroom right next to an elevator shaft, your kitchen, a party wall, or your entrance. Save the best window views for the living areas.

◆ **Whatever room is used the most should have the best view.** If you're constantly in the kitchen and this is where your guests all congregate, make sure it's open to both your central living space and windows.

◆ **Keep in mind what you will be looking at when in your rooms.** If possible, visit your loft when your preliminary layout is done, armed with a tape measure and chalk. Calculate the location of each designated area and chalk the outline on the floor, then stand in each space. Look around and make sure you like what you see.

◆ **Consider varying the floor levels.** Kitchens should have a maximum rise of only two or three steps, so you're not hauling groceries up and down stairs. Elevated offices, gyms, or master bedrooms afford you some privacy and a bird's-eye view of your domain. The cavity created underneath will never go to waste because it can always be utilized for storage. Appropriate some of the air space for a second floor where ceiling heights are 17 feet (5.2 meters) or more.

◆ **Don't forget to allow for storage.** Most loft buildings have lockers for your use but they're not as convenient as space in your own unit.

◆ **Start by locating the entrance on your plan,** then put in the spaces most important to you. For example, if you definitely must have a king-size bed, allot enough space to accommodate it. Everyone's priorities are different; I interviewed a fellow in Manhattan who didn't have a kitchen. His reasoning was: "What possible need would I have for a kitchen when I'm surrounded by the most eclectic and superb restaurants in the world?"

◆ **Go back to your initial list** and see what functional areas you use the most. That should be your guide. I've provided a *chart of the necessities* for you to refer to.

The Necessities

Doors: Entrance 3'o" (.9 m); Interior 2'6" (.8 m)

Walls: Allow 6" (152 mm)

Closets: 2'6" (.8 m) wide minimum by 2'o" (.6 m) deep

Walk-in-closets: With hanging on one side only 5'o" (1.5 m) wide by any length; With hanging on both sides 7'o" (2.1 m) wide by any length

Passageways: Allow 4'o" (1.2 m)

Around furniture: Allow 2'6" (.8 m) to 3'o" (.9 m)

Toilet: Allow 3'o" (.9 m)

Bathtub: Allow 5'o" (1.5 m) long by 2'6" (.8 m) wide

Bathroom vanities: 1'9" (.6 m) deep x any length x 2'6" (.8 m) high

Kitchen counters: 2'o" (.6 m) deep x any length x 3'o" high

Standard refrigerator: 2'6" (.8 m) wide x 2'7" (.8 m) deep

Stove: 2'6" (.8 m) wide by 2'o" (.6 m) deep

Dishwasher: 2'o" (.6 m) wide by 2'o" (.6 m) deep

Two-bowl kitchen sink: 2'8" (.9 m) wide

Queen bed: 5'o" (1.5 m) wide by 6'o" (1.8 m) long

King bed: 6'o" (1.8 m) wide by 7'o" (2.1 m) long

‹ Elevated areas segment the space without the use of definitive drywall partitions. If you work from home and receive clients, locate the office near the entrance to maintain privacy in your living space.

entertaining. Closets built into the walls, or functioning *as* walls, disappear when invisible hardware is used. These cavities can conceal workstations or storage with art mounted to the face; adjoining recesses can display sculpture or a functional built-in entry table.

On the other hand, by designing a small, intimate vestibule—even going so far as to add a dropped ceiling—a smaller loft will seem much larger by comparison, and will shock the visitor by the contradiction.

Coat storage can take the form of a traditional drywall box or more casual means such as coat trees or pegs. You can also play with stud space (the area behind the face drywall between the two supports) if there is no insulation there. Hooks can be recessed into this cavity for

◆ **If you're unsure of the dimensions you're allotting,** measure what you have now, or a friend's space if you admire the size of their rooms. This will help you to envision what you're mapping out. Throughout this planning process, close your eyes and try to envision what you've planned. Picture yourself in the area and do a 360-degree turn. Do you like what you see? If not, change it now.

◆ **Entryways.** Okay, so we've entered your loft. What do we need here? A place for coats, hats, umbrellas, keys, purses, a mirror to make sure there's no lipstick on your teeth before you hit the street.

In a large loft, entertaining on a grand scale predicates an area for the arrival of several people at one time and their incumbent outerwear. This doesn't have to be wasted square footage when you're not a less cluttered look, or the area can become the receptacle for a full-length mirror, shelves, or console shelf.

◆ **In lofts where the floor is beyond salvation,** turn the situation to your advantage by elevating the new floor. Stepping up from an entrance creates a sense of arrival and expectation, especially in smaller lofts where space is at a premium. The void below the raised floor will facilitate plumbing runs and access to them.

◆ **A powder room is the perfect accompaniment to the foyer.** It can be miniscule, as long as it accommodates a sink and toilet. Finishing touches will give even the tiniest room pizzazz. For a **guest bathroom,** size the room based on a tub/shower combination, the most practical solution, or a separate shower stall, which can take up less room.

◆ **The master bathroom,** or *ensuite* as it's also known, is an area that requires some privacy and functional details. For the basic floor plan, include only the necessities, then customize the space when we look at bathrooms in detail (see page 69). Locate the *ensuite* next to the master bedroom for private access.

> *Take into account unique characteristics that can be incorporated into the plan such as steel beamed ceilings, freight elevators, and exposed ducts. Columns are one of the most defining details of lofts and as such should be showcased.*

◆ **The kitchen** is generally the most detailed expanse in residences. As with the bathroom, include only the necessities at first: refrigerator, stove, sink, and counters. Details should be added later (see page 45). Basic dimensions are charted on page 51.

◆ **The remaining space** will be used for the bedroom, living room, dining room, and a guestroom (if desired). At this point, you should also add any large items to the plan, such as my baby grand piano and king-size bed (see page 68).

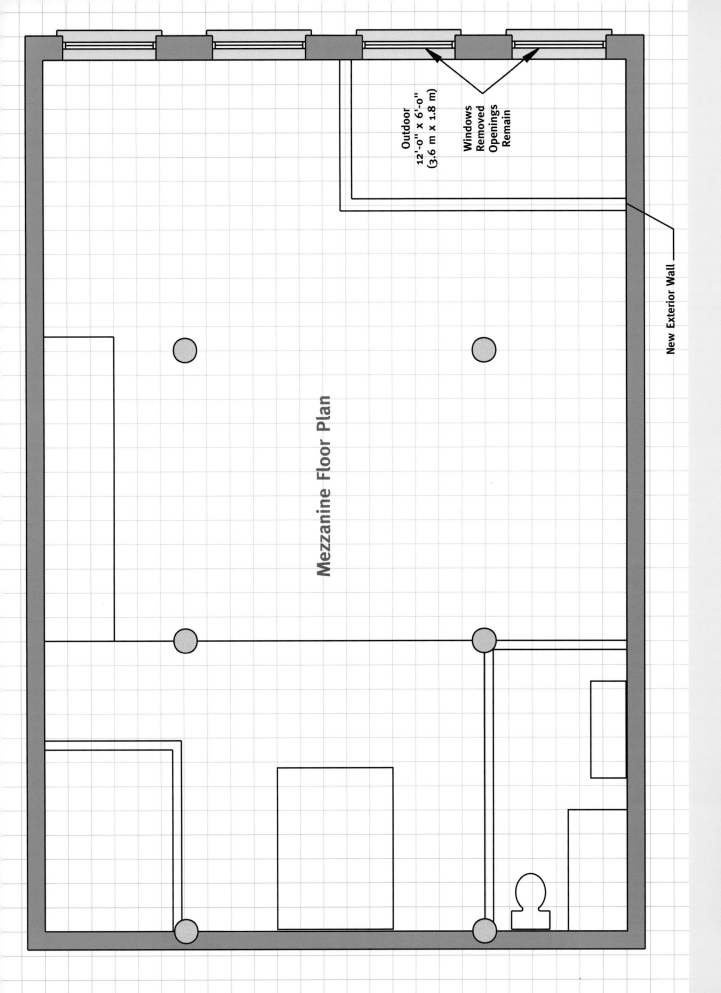

Outdoor
12'-0" x 6'-0"
(3.6 m x 1.8 m)

Windows
Removed
Openings
Remain

New Exterior Wall

Mezzanine Floor Plan

A Basic Floor Plan

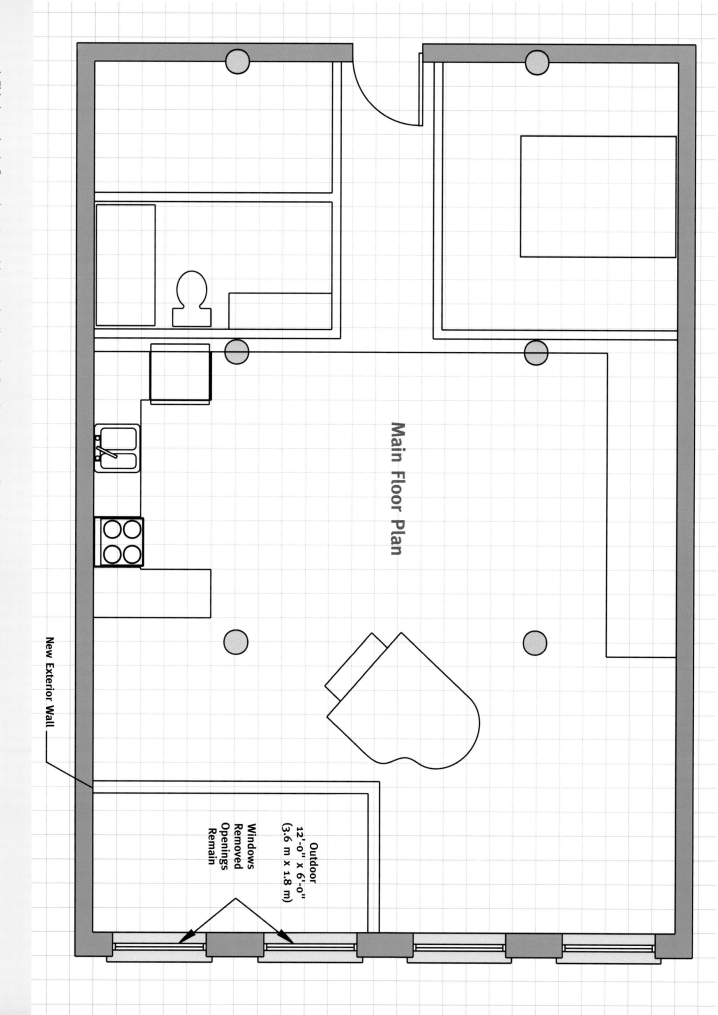

Main Floor Plan

Outdoor
12'-0" x 6'-0"
(3.6 m x 1.8 m)

Windows
Removed
Openings
Remain

New Exterior Wall

∧ This is my basic floor plan. As I add more details and refine the space, you'll see that it will constantly evolve, right up to and including the construction period when unknown factors may force me to alter the design.

< This beautiful loft is well-suited to hosting parties. An island on wheels is easily rolled away when you need the space for large gatherings. Or, you can pull the fabric partition to hide the kitchen and create a more intimate space to gather with a few close friends.

> Floating below the ceiling, the freestanding cabinets screen the kitchen functions while maintaining the flowing openness that defines lofts.

Kitchens

The kitchen is usually the most detailed and expensive space in your loft. It takes considerable thought to produce an efficient working kitchen, and believe it or not, it's a very personal space. Before you begin your design, write down what you want your kitchen to do, how you've used your kitchen in the past, and what you see as your kitchen's place in the new scenario. Fill out the chart on the next page to help define your needs and wants.

for you

What Do You Need?

	YESTERDAY	LAST WEEK	FOUR MONTHS	LAST YEAR
Did I Bake?				
Did I Make a Meal?				
Coffeemaker				
Toaster				
Cooktop				
Oven				
Microwave				
Refrigerator				
BBQ/Grill				
Dishwasher				
Ice Cubes				
Chopping Block				

What Do You Want?

☐
☐
☐
☐
☐
☐
☐
☐
☐
☐
☐
☐

for me

What Do I Need?

	YESTERDAY	LAST WEEK	FOUR MONTHS	LAST YEAR
Did I Bake?			6	
Did I Make a Meal?	X	4	17	72
Coffeemaker	X	5	96	264
Toaster		3	48	132
Cooktop		4	72	176
Oven		1	16	44
Microwave		2	32	88
Refrigerator	X	7	124	352
BBQ/Grill	X	2	32	88
Dishwasher	X	3	48	176
Ice Cubes			4	26
Chopping Block		5	96	264

What Do I Want?

☑ Meal preparation space
☑ Accommodation for caterers
☑ Coffeemaker
☑ Toaster oven
☑ Combination microwave/oven
☑ Refrigerator/freezer with ice cube maker
☑ Outdoor barbecue
☑ Dishwasher
☑ Compactor
☑ Food disposer
☑ Chopping block
☑ Cooktop with warming element

What Do I Need? What Do I Want?

Your selections will impact the size and layout. A person who bakes or prepares meals from raw materials requires more counter space, a larger sink to handle cookie trays and roasting pans, and maybe an additional sink for vegetable preparation. Do you want a cozy spot for casual dining at a table or will eating side-by-side at a counter suffice?

Refer to the "needs" list you just filled out. How many times did you entertain in the past year? Once or on a regular basis? This is one factor that will alter your kitchen plan dramatically. Your basic day-to-day needs may be as nominal as a coffeemaker and a refrigerator to keep your cream in, but cooking for friends or family may be an important part of your life, even if it is only several times a year. For yearly gatherings, I recommend a catering service. Don't laugh—you'll be able to do this for many years before the cost equals the additional equipment you would have to buy.

From my chart, I can ascertain that my priorities are a coffeemaker, a toaster, a cooktop, a refrigerator, a chopping block, and a dishwasher. I don't need a full freezer, or at least not one in the kitchen proper. I barbeque a lot, so an inside grill or a protected location outside would be great.

> *If cooking is your passion, you should consider incorporating a large, professional hood vent and cook top into your kitchen layout.*

Planning for Change

It's obvious from my wants and needs assessment that I entertain nominally, but I know that I enjoy hosting events and hope to do more if I ever have more time, and that I do host catered events occasionally.

Now it's time for the hard part—step away from yourself, and be honest. Our needs change as our lives change. I used to love the advance preparation for a party as much as the event itself—rifling through cookbooks, deciding the menu, gathering the groceries, developing a theme, preparing the food. The problem was, I was usually exhausted by the time the guests arrived. Like many people, I tried to do everything myself and be a "super-woman." When I joined my guests for a cocktail, I was likely to forget the salad in the fridge, or the dessert course, having skipped meals and sleep in preparation for the event. I hated the last minute prep, the serving, and the cleanup, because this was when my guests were most available for visiting and I wanted to be with them, not be a scullery maid.

So to be honest with myself, I can admit that I now enjoy hosting more than the accolades I received from cooking. And even if I do all the arrangements for the event, including cooking, I would rather have others do the final preparation (putting the food onto the plates, the last minute cooking, the serving) and cleanup. With that in mind, I've put together a kitchen for myself that will allow me to cook nominally on a regular basis, accommodate guests during preparation if I do decide to cook, and be serviceable to caterers.

< A loft that revels in its past!

Towering concrete columns are circled with spotlights and a wooden ladder accesses upper storage, but our eyes are drawn to the glistening salvaged stainless steel cooler doors that encase the upper kitchen cabinets.

17 Basic Tips for Kitchen Planning

1 Allow yourself as much **counter space** as possible.

2 **Separate appliances** with countertops.

3 If you entertain often, **consider a commercial cooler** instead of a traditional refrigerator. The uninterrupted expanse of shelves is perfect for holding platters of food and cases of drinks.

4 **Wall ovens are a luxury for large kitchens.** They occupy valuable counter space.

5 **Drawers** make items more accessible than cupboards.

6 **Drawers** cost twice as much as cupboards.

7 The more **built-ins** you install, the more limited you will be as your needs change.

8 **Cooktop grills** need efficient exhaust fans, otherwise everything in your loft will be covered with grease.

9 Allow for **easy access** of items used on a regular basis.

10 House **dishes** within close range of the dishwasher.

11 Prioritize **storage.** Deeper shelves above upper cabinets are ideal for seldom used serving dishes.

12 Consider **air space** in the design. It could be used for a hanging pot rack or ladder accessible storage (see above), leaving your arm's length areas for day-to-day use.

13 **Screen the mess.** Open kitchens are great, but you may want to mask the preparation from your dining view.

14 **Position** the kitchen close to your entrance so you don't have far to transport groceries.

15 If your kitchen is on a different level, **limit the number of steps** to two risers.

16 Remember that **seating at a counter** requires an overhang for knee space.

17 **Find the components that meet your needs.** Kitchens have become such big business of late that there is an appliance out there to do the most mundane of functions. The choices are unbelievable, as are the range of costs.

Refrigerators and freezers can be as small as a single dresser drawer or as large as the commercial cooler at your convenience store. For the wine connoisseur, there are individual temperature-controlled units replicating the caves at vineyards. The serious collector can designate space anywhere in the loft and create their personal cellar. Even an insulated closet will suffice. Compact mechanics sized to fit the area will maintain the air at a constant temperature and humidity. Pea gravel on the floor can serve the dual purpose of capturing moisture while hopefully saving the odd bottle that slips from your grasp. Cocktail drinkers can experience the delight of **icemakers** that guarantee single, clear cubes every time, going so far as to replace stored cubes after a predetermined period. You'll never have to suffer the indignity of frost or that insidious taste of old ice. Anything is possible.

From an installation perspective, kitchen equipment often requires specialized plumbing, wiring, or ventilation. You may want the convenience of having your espresso machine hooked up directly to the water and drainage. Mark the model numbers on your plan for the plumber and electrician to refer to, or go one step further by adding pertinent information on separate mechanical and electrical plans. A **basic mechanical plan** is a copy of the floor plan detailing the location of plumbing, plumbing fixtures, heating, and air conditioning. The **electrical plan** indicates the location and electrical requirements—volts and watts (see page 146–147).

> A subtle departure from the behemoths of old, refrigerator drawers can be installed to dispense food where it's needed, be it by the stove, sink, chopping block, dining area—or all of the above!

< The industrial heritage of lofts is reflected in the adaptation of commercial equipment to residential use. Glass doors on refrigerators transform food from mere sustenance to a design accessory by adding color and texture to the kitchen interior.

Power Play—Appliances

Research appliances before you start space planning. You may be surprised at some of the innovations and the impact they will have on your decisions. For example, in my loft I'm going to reduce the amount of planned storage space for dishes. I can either install a **dishwasher** with drawers, or install two full-size dishwashers—I'll simply rotate the dishes from one unit to the next as they're used.

Convection ovens that also function as microwaves are another space saver. Refer to the interior dimension of ovens—most European models are more compact than their North American counterparts. If you only need an oven for cooking turkey once or twice a year, maybe a quality toaster oven would suffice, and you can find an alternative way to roasting the bird. It makes more sense to heat as small a cavity as possible; on a regular basis I use my compact toaster oven to bake potatoes, cook casseroles, and broil steaks. My butcher is happy to cook my holiday turkey on his commercial spit for a nominal price, probably less than the power used to operate my oven.

Clients with **warming drawers** swear by them—the adjustable humidity controls keep food appropriately moist or crisp until it's ready to serve. Or maybe a wood-burning oven, like the El Forno, is your idea of heaven. Refuse to automatically accept the norm and instead customize to suit your needs now and in the foreseeable future.

Kitchen Appliances and Fixtures

		MINIMUM	MAXIMUM
Refrigerator	w.	2' (.60 m)	4' (1.21 m)
	d.	2' (.60 m)	2'9" (.83 m)
	h.	5'4" (1.62 m)	7' (2.13 m)
Undercounter Single Door Units	w.	2'3" (.68 m)	3'0" (.91 m)
	d.	1'10" (.55 m)	2' (.60 m)
	h.	2'4" (.71 m)	2'11" (.88 m)
Undercounter Refrigeration Drawers	w.	2' (.60 m)	2' (.60 m)
	d.	2' (.60 m)	2' (.60 m)
	h.	2'10" (.86 m)	2'10" (.86 m)
Automatic Ice-Cube Maker	w.	1'2" (.35 m)	1'6" (.45 m)
	d.	1'6" (.45 m)	2' (.60 m)
	h.	2' (.60 m)	2'10" (.86 m)
Wine Coolers	w.	2' (.60 m)	2'6" (.76 m)
	d.	2' (.60 m)	2' (.60 m)
	h.	2'10" (.86 m)	7'0" (2.13 m)
Commercial Coolers	w.	2'1" (.63 m)	6'6" (1.98 m)
	d.	1'11" (.58 m)	2'8" (.81 m)
	h.	5'4" (1.62 m)	7'2" (2.13 m)
Cooktops	w.	1'3" (.38 m)	5' (1.52 m)
	d.	1'8" (.50 m)	2' (.60 m)
	h.	2" (.05 m)	8" (.20 m)
Ovens (Single)	w.	2' (.60 m)	2'6" (.76 m)
	d.	1'5" (.43 m)	2'2" (.66 m)
	h.	1'4" (.40 m)	2'7" (.78 m)
Ovens (Double)	w.	2' (.60 m)	2'6" (.76 m)
	d.	2' (.60 m)	2'2" (.66 m)
	h.	4' (1.21 m)	4'8" (1.42 m)
Warming Drawer	w.	2' (.60 m)	2'6" (.76 m)
	d.	1'10" (.55 m)	2' (.60 m)
	h.	10" (.25 m)	1' (.02 m)
Microwave Ovens	w.	1'10" (.55 m)	2'6" (.76 m)
	d.	1'4" (.40 m)	2' (.60 m)
	h.	1'1" (.33 m)	1'5" (.43 m)
Single Bowl Sinks	w.	10" (.25 m)	2'6" (.76 m)
	d.	1'3" (.38 m)	2'2" (.66 m)
	h.	5" (.12 m)	1' (.30 m)
Double Bowl Sinks	w.	2' (.60 m)	4'2" (1.2 m)
	d.	1'6" (.45 m)	2'2" (.66 m)
	h.	6" (.15 m)	1' (.30 m)

		MINIMUM	MAXIMUM
Triple Bowl Sinks	w.	3'2" (.96 m)	5' (1.52 m)
	d.	1'8" (.50 m)	2'2" (.66 m)
	h.	6" (.15 m)	1' (.30 m)
Dishwashers	w.	2' (.60 m)	2' (.60 m)
	d.	1'11" (.58 m)	2' (.60 m)
	h.	1'6" (.45 m)	3' (.91 m)
Trash Compactors	w.	1' (.30 m)	1'6" (.45 m)
	d.	1'6" (.45 m)	2' (.60 m)
	h.	2'10" (.86 m)	2'10" (.86 m)
Disposers	dia.	.6" (.15 m)	1' (.30 m)
	h.	1' (.30 m)	1'6" (.45 m)

> Compact dishwasher drawers can supplement a full-size unit for delicate glassware when entertaining, augment a bar, or efficiently handle the nominal china of urban dwellers where eating out is irresistible.

General Notes: Sizes are nominal; fractions were raised to the next whole number. This is a sampling of sizes. New additions hit the market regularly. European models are more compact with a smaller capacity but are more energy efficient. Dimensions are for both electric and gas appliances.

Workflow should move from the refrigerator to the sink, to the range, and finally to the serving area. The total length from start to finish should average less than 23 lineal feet (7.01 m) and not exceed 26 lineal feet (7.92).

Refrigeration Notes: Allow 1'3" (.38 m) minimum counter space at latch side of door for loading. Allow a minimum of 1'6" (.46 m) between latch side of door and a turn in the counter. The most convenient location for the refrigerator is closest to the entry. Allow storage for other grocery items in close proximity. Dimensions refer to individual refrigerators and freezers as well as combination units.

Ranges/Cooktops Notes: Allow 1'6" (.45 m) to 2' (.60 m) of counter space on one side of range. Allow minimum of 1'2" (.35 m) between the center of an element and a turn in the counter. Allow 3' (.91 m) to 3'6" (1.06 m) between the range and nearest piece of equipment. Store pots, pans, cooking utensils, seasonings, and serving dishes nearby.

Sinks Notes: Allow 1'6" (0.75 m) to 3' (0.91 m) counter space on one side of sink. Allow 2' (.60 m) to 3' (.91 m) counter space on other side of sink. Allow a minimum of 1'2" (0.35 m) between the center of the sink bowl and a turn in the counter. As the sink's function is common to both the refrigerator and the range, the most convenient location is between them. Provide storage for everyday dishes, pots, and pans in close proximity. Dimensions above are for bar, laundry, and kitchen sinks.

Dishwasher Notes: Drawer units now available with each drawer of maximum two 2'w x 2'd x 1'6"h (.60 m x .60 m x.45 m).

Disposers Note: Attach to the drain below one sink. Very little space will be lost if the drain is located at the back of the sink. Noise is their biggest drawback. Look for units with sound insulation.

Waterworks

No kitchen is complete without a **sink**, and the choices available in regard to size, finish, and style demand careful consideration. It's actually easier if you're on a restricted budget. The reliable double bowl stainless steel sink is hard to beat for cost effectiveness, durability, longevity, and size options. When purchasing, you'll see a number rating such as 18-8 or 18-10. This means that it is 18 percent chromium to give it a brilliant sparkle and 8 percent or 10 percent nickel, the higher the better, to provide strength and protect against rust and corrosion.

When selecting a kitchen sink, be sure to note the bottom inside dimension; this is the actual useable space. The widest outside measurements are listed by manufacturers and include the mounting edge, so if you're selecting a sink based on this size to accommodate your baking trays you'll be disappointed when they don't fit. Sinks with vertical walls maximize space, and drains positioned at the back of the sink leave more useable space underneath.

Think about how you cook (or don't, as the case may be). If you bake or roast often, a two-bowl sink with one side designed to accommodate large roasting pans or cookie sheets or a large single bowl would be best. Many companies have reintroduced sinks with attached drain boards, a common item before dishwashers became popular. If you don't need two sinks but do accumulate dishes that require hand washing, this is a good alternative that frees up more under counter space.

Do you want a **garbage disposer**, and will your local code allow you to have one? If you install one, make sure it has its own separate sink in addition to the wash and drain sink. I opted for a two-bowl sink with one large bowl and one standard size that I use for drying hand washables. My disposal was installed in the sink outfitted with a draining rack. I discovered that the two functions were incompatible. Both were used the most when we were entertaining, but the trouble was with a draining rack full of crystal glasses, gold rimmed china, or silver cutlery that couldn't go in the dishwasher, the disposer beneath was inaccessible. Live and learn.

The options available with residential sinks are considerable. Removable **chopping blocks, colanders,** and **drainage racks** custom sized to fit over a sink allow for easy drainage of wet foods and dishes. Cut-outs in the sink surface allow for easy disposal of food refuse through a chute to a bin in the cabinet below. So many choices can be daunting but the wide price range will help you narrow the field. Price is often related more to style than quality. Cast iron sinks appear affluent and substantial but are susceptible to scratches, staining, and chipping. Unless that worn look appeals to you or you have the means to replace the sink after a few years, it may not be the right choice.

< Sink modules sit right on the kitchen cabinet and eliminate the need for complicated sink cut-outs. Separate compartments provide areas and accessories that facilitate food preparation. The square lines and narrow edge overhang are simple yet tailored, a compliment to Spartan kitchens in "open concept" living situations.

Three Sink Options

Sinks come in three formats: with **rims, undermount, or continuous with the counter.** The standard is the **sink with a rim,** or edge, that sits on top of the counter material. This is the least expensive because it's easy to install, and allows for a margin of error in the countertop cutout. This type of sink is a prerequisite for plastic laminate countertops, and it can also be used with just about every other material. Have your sink on site when your countertop is being installed, or at least the template that manufacturers supply, so the contractor knows the exact size and can position it correctly.

Undermount sinks have no exposed upper edges and are installed under the countertop material. They exude a very custom appearance, sitting below a finished edge of stone. If you want that look but can't afford the expensive countertop they require, use sink rings—hardware that allows you to use undermount sinks with inexpensive plastic laminate or tile countertops. Bonus.

< A corner sink on an island is accessible and functional from both sides. The two-bowl layout with integrated dish drainer and vegetable strainer is the optimum setup for the installation of a food disposer. Installed under one of the sink drains, the other functions can operate unimpeded.

∧ A circular set of sink and matching drainer may not meet all your cleanup needs, but as a supplementary unit on an island to prep vegetables, it's an attractive addition. The affordable cost of stainless steel lets you splurge on extras.

Continuous sinks are just that—one-piece sink and countertop combinations manufactured using one type of material. In commercial installations, they are typically made of stainless steel; in residences, man-made materials such as Corian are often used.

What about **custom-made sinks?** Welding a stainless steel basin and backsplash together creates a sleek unit that won't leak. Contact restaurant suppliers or sheet metal workers in your area for fabrication prices—you may be surprised at how inexpensive they are.

Sandstone sinks have a rustic appeal. They can be custom made from a template you provide that indicates the length, width, and depth of the sink; they're delivered in five pieces—the bottom with a hole for the drain, and four sides. Construct a plywood base to support the sink.

^ A traditional two-bowl sink with spillway—the lowered separation bar between—and attached drain board takes on a contemporary look when manufactured in a combination of man-made and natural products (in this case resin and granite).

> With not a cupboard door or countertop in sight, this European kitchen is a complete departure from tradition. Except for the cooktop and sink unit, everything is mobile; you can literally take the kitchen with you when you move.

∨ Manufacturers have come up with snappy designs for liquid soap dispensers that look quite at home beside an ergonomic faucet.

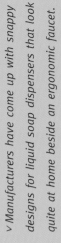

∧ With a curvaceous gooseneck, this single hole deck-mount faucet presents an interesting architectural profile to complement its functionality.

∨ A single lever mixer that provides both hot and cold water is the optimum for ease of operation. With a pullout hand spray and removable aerator, the performance belies an inconspicuous design.

Fittings: Faucets and Taps

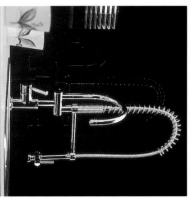

Faucets and taps are known as **fittings** to the trade. The water delivery system is called a **faucet**. The individual units that activate the flow of hot or cold water are called **taps**, and a single unit that combines both functions is a **mixer**. Look at taps and faucets from both the aesthetic and the practical point of view. Single lever faucets are very efficient, but expensive. Do you need a sprayer to rinse dishes, water plants, or fill tall vases? Sprayer alternatives include extendable and gooseneck faucets. Unless the faucet is mounted separately on the countertop or wall behind the sink, it must be compatible with your predrilled sink holes. Confirm the need for a deck plate that is often installed underneath faucets and taps, and coordinate the sink strainers that fit over your drain to the sink, not the faucets.

Fittings are one area where you definitely get what you pay for. Whenever I have skimped on the cost of fittings, I have lived to regret it. I don't care what the manufacturer's warranty says, they will fight to the death to escape replacing a unit that doesn't function as advertised, leaving you to decide if it's even worth the effort to recoup your losses. Spend the money up front and it will be one less thing you have to think about. Look for fittings with nickel undercoating or triple plating to protect against corrosion. White composite units tend to yellow; beige or black are more reliable choices.

< From behind the scenes at your favorite restaurant to front and center in your loft kitchen, a towering, commercially inspired sprayer packs a design punch.

Fitting Finishes

Do your price comparisons on the basic chrome finish that is ironically the most inexpensive, reliable, and practical from a maintenance point of view. Your choice will always boil down to personal priorities. In my kitchen, I opted for the impractical porcelain sink in black because aesthetically it looked best with a black slate counter and antique copper taps. The sink shows scratches, the slate requires periodic sealing, and I have to coat the French antique copper taps with petroleum jelly to protect the finish, but it looks good to me. What can I say?

◆ **Stainless steel and nickel finishes** are much more expensive, but they have a richer (pardon the pun) depth of color and softer aesthetic with the same practicality and reliability.

◆ **Solid brass or copper,** even when coated with epoxy or lacquer, will tarnish over time in the joints or where water makes contact. If you keep coming back to either choice even after you know their downfalls, consider uncoated fixtures that will last indefinitely. While you will have to polish occasionally, the soft patina that will develop over time will offset your efforts.

◆ **Twenty-four karat gold** is even more delicate than treated brass, demanding gentle use and care, something difficult to ensure if you have others handling the maintenance. From personal experience, I know that even over-spray from nonabrasive sink cleaners can damage the protective finish when used on a regular basis.

◆ **Electrostatic plating** can produce any finish imaginable from antique copper to bronze, but once again, longevity and ease of maintenance are problematic. Those of you in the position to replace your fittings every few years can select virtually any finish from a reputable line. If you have better things to do with your time or money than maintaining and replacing fittings, stick with the silver finishes—chrome, stainless steel, or nickel.

< The simple addition of black rubber detailing on the faucet and mixer lever elevate this unit to prominence against the stainless steel surroundings.

Tips on Tops

The next decision confronting you will be the countertop material. Like the cabinets they cap and the sinks they surround, counters range from utilitarian plastic laminate to exotic stone, with a cost variance to match. Unless you're set on the streamlined, sleek appearance, the best result is often a combination of materials.

◆ **Plastic laminate** countertops are a good choice when you have budgetary restraints. The choices available are unbelievable, and often the simulated stone, granite, and slate finishes are indistinguishable from the real thing, and as an all-purpose surface it performs well: It won't easily scorch if a hot pot is set to rest on it for a short period of time; the suede finish can hide fingerprints and the odd knife cut; and it's easy to clean, inexpensive, and will keep looking good for a reasonable length of time.

◆ **Stone** has become a sought after countertop surface with the most common choices being slate, marble, limestone, and granite. Stone is naturally very dull and rough. Polishing the surface creates varying degrees of sheen to suit your taste. A tumbled surface, most commonly used on marbles and limestone, has the most matte finish. A honed surface is smooth with a soft patina that gives a casual, understated look. Stone is sold as a slab—a section of quarried stone that is large enough to cover several feet without a seem. Make the most of your investment by hand selecting your slabs; stone is a natural product and the variations of pattern and color can be quite different from the original sample.

‹ Size the height of cabinets to suit your physique; this is easy to do prior to construction. Dimensions shown are standard heights and separating distances for base cabinets with deep profile, open shelves above.

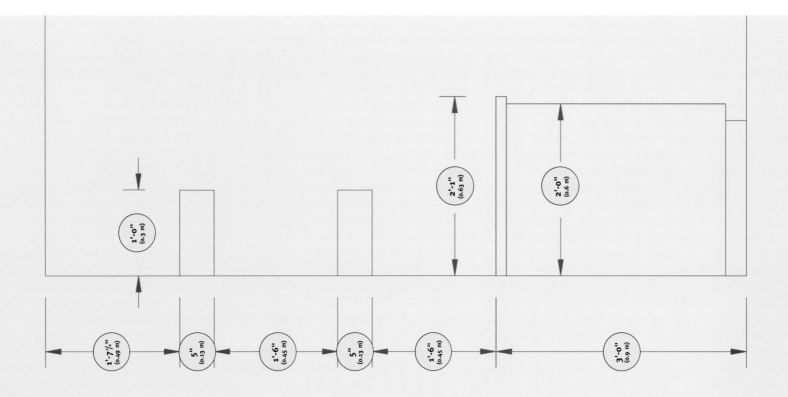

Stone tiles are much more affordable than slabs, because they are thinner and every remnant can be cut into sellable pieces, providing quite a range of sizes to chose from. Remember to factor in the cost of a finished edge for stone tile, an item which is sold separately. Intricate edge moldings that run the length of the countertop can make up the difference between tile and slab. Wall tiles are designed for vertical surfaces only because they won't stand up to pressure of any kind or the more intense wear and tear of daily use.

◆ Creating **concrete** countertops can be a detailed, time-consuming process with few guarantees, and contractor's prices are right up there with stone. Installed over a wood base, the concrete is reinforced for structural strength with steel or wire mesh, and additives like acrylic, small stones, or crushed glass are added for subtle variations in texture. A dam edge is screwed into the wood base to keep

the concrete in place until it's set, and then the dam is removed. For a warmer appearance other than the natural gray, chemical stains can be applied with varying results, depending on the curing time of the slab, the composition of the concrete, and the presence of surface materials such as dust, grease, or oil. However, if you have your heart set on a very specific color, another surface would be more reliable. Concrete is porous, so apply several coats of a good sealer (such as epoxy) after the material has cured to prevent staining.

◆ **Ceramic tile** is another counter option; it's installed the same way as stone tiles with all the same problems and advantages. Floor tiles are best because they are thick and strong. Kitchen counter tiles should be impervious to moisture, with an absorption rate of .05 percent or less. Porcelain tiles fall into this category.

Installing Countertops

The **standard height** of a counter is 36 inches (914 mm). Make sure this suits your stature, as most cabinets can be *easily* raised or lowered a few inches in the manufacturing or installation stage, and it can make a world of difference to your back. Also consider at what height you're most comfortable chopping, baking, and cooking food on range top, as these are also the functions that benefit from specialized counter surfaces. They can be lowered and still look appropriate.

Installation varies with the material. Thick slab countertops can float on top of a wood or steel support system, but are more susceptible to cracking if put under direct pressure—such as someone hoisting themselves up to sit on the counter. A more sound installation option is to cement the tiles or slab on a stable deck. This is usually ½-inch (13 mm) number one grade plywood screwed onto a wood frame every 2 inches (51 mm) to remove any possibly of the wood twisting or warping.

Grout fills the gaps between the slab pieces or tiles. It is porous and will absorb liquids, which may cause stains—darker colors will conceal stains more effectively. Be sure to apply grout sealer on a regular basis, which will help repel stains as well. Epoxy grouts are more stain-resistant but also more expensive and difficult to apply. Be sure to consider the thickness of the grout line—from the barely discernible ¹⁄₁₆ inch (1.5 mm) to ½ inch (13 mm), which will create a distinct outline between each tile. If you're installing tile yourself, grout guides are available to ensure a consistent distance between pieces.

^ *Solid surface materials, such as Corian, are man-made from combinations of various polymers. Smooth to the touch with a low-luster patina, it has a translucent quality. Big advantages are the seamless appearance from the junctions to the edge details, stain resistance due to the nonporous composition, and reparablity because of the color-through characteristic. The cost is comparable to stone.*

∧ It's hard to beat the economics of plastic laminate countertops. New photo-imaging techniques make it visually difficult to discern from the natural materials they imitate.

< *A new twist on the backsplash, stainless steel tiles distract your eye from minor scratches and flaws with the appealing refraction and diffusion of light.*

Backsplashes

A backsplash refers to any wall behind a countertop. Except for the area behind a range top, which demands a heat resistant backsplash, the possibilities are endless. It can extend continuously from the countertop in the same material for a classic look, be in contrast, or have an illusory affect.

Your choice of **finish** should be predicated on how you use the kitchen and your personal temperament. Shiny surfaces such as **mirror, stainless steel,** or **solid colors in paint or tile** will add depth, luminescence, and animation, especially when illuminated with concealed lighting from above or below. However they will also prominently display every splatter and splash. For the fastidious, a better option in a well-used kitchen would be surfaces with textural or color differences. An excellent compromise is **clear glass panels** applied over a painted wall, or the glass itself painted or etched on the back before installation. The eye is drawn to the background texture or color of the paint, reducing the prominence of marks on the reflective surface. Consequently you attain all the subtle advantages of a shiny material without the constant upkeep.

Stylish Storage

There are three basic groups of cabinets available. The most affordable cabinetry is **factory made** in a limited range of sizes and finishes. The frame, drawers, and shelving are called carcasses, and are purchased separately from the drawer and door faces that are screwed on. Both are manufactured from medium density fiberboard (MDF), an amalgam of paper that has plastic laminate, wood veneer, or a paint finish applied to the exterior. It's a structurally sound material that doesn't warp; it's only drawback is that any dings to the surface are difficult to repair and can reveal the inner core of fiber.

A step up from MDF are **custom** kitchens with factory made interior components. The carcasses are still composite boards but the exterior face material includes solid wood as well as the choices listed above. Although the sizes available are still finite, there are more to choose from and they can be modified to fit your circumstance. Stock storage systems such as pullout bins and wire baskets can also be incorporated. Finally, there's the completely custom kitchen, which is built from scratch both inside and out, to suit your design. Generally **handmade** from solid wood, your imagination is the only thing limiting the components and the exterior finish.

Companies such as Ikea have great looking kitchens waiting for you to install. With all the components sold separately, it's easy to design a kitchen that will be uniquely yours at a fraction of the cost of custom manufacturing. Stand base cabinets on furniture legs or an open-faced metal plinth (a shallow box, open top and bottom) to raise them off the floor. Replace the central panel of doors with glass, wire mesh, or fiberglass screening. Alternative hardware could be smooth beach stones you've collected or miscellaneous cutlery. Have holes drilled to accommodate the necessary mounting hardware. Play with the hanging of upper cabinets by staggering their height and leaving some open compartments.

The key to a cabinet's longevity is the **operating hardware**, so check that out before making your decision. Do the drawers run smoothly on metal glides? Are the doors installed with adjustable metal hinges? Visit the manufacturer's showroom and see how the floor models have held up.

> *Look for companies that sell components separately. You can easily mix and match pieces to suit your style and kitchen needs, thereby giving yourself the tailored fit of handmade without the higher cost.*

∧ Materials speak volumes in this loft kitchen. Bamboo envelopes the ceiling and custom cabinets for a rich counterpoint to the concrete floor and island countertop. The unified stainless steel backsplash, sink, and countertop in the prep area come alive with illumination, augmenting the seamless, pristine interior.

Style

When selecting **finishes** for surfaces in your kitchen, think about how you will be using the space, what kind of exposure it will have, and how it will interact in the loft. Glossy surfaces such as stainless steel will show every fingerprint; not a great idea if you have children or cook a lot. Dark finishes show dust and grease marks even with normal use. A glossy white kitchen next to an expanse of windows with a southern exposure will be blinding.

Style Tips

If your kitchen is open to other areas, treat it as furniture. It will have a huge presence, so visualize the finished product in the space. In a formal, traditional interior you may want the kitchen to continue this aesthetic. Rich cherry wood cabinets with fine detailing and cornice molding would complement the space; or you may want to contrast the setting with a modern stainless steel kitchen that reflects the industrial roots of the building. Both would be appropriate, but what appeals to you?

Kitchen settings don't have to be a vista of wrap-around matching cabinets. Practicality and ease of use should always take precedence over aesthetics in the kitchen, but you can achieve a happy median. Consider a run of cabinets broken by an old armoire that houses dishes. Typesetter's cabinets are ideal for storing spices and cutlery. Nursery school locker racks with their individual removable bins make an eclectic pantry. Each bin can hold products of the same kind: one for cereal, baking goods, pasta, etc., so that when you want to make a selection, you remove the whole container.

> The sum of my kitchen triangle dimensions is an acceptable 16 feet (4.9 meters). I've flanked my sink with two dishwashers—since I don't display my china, I'm going to reduce the amount of storage I need by simply transferring dishes from one unit to another as they're used.

The What, Where, & Wise

Efficient kitchen planning is dependent on the proximity of the primary functional elements. Our goal is for a layout that looks impressive while conserving your energy. I've been called in to redesign new kitchens that encompassed so much space that the owner was exhausted by the time a meal had been prepped, presented, and cleaned up.

The kitchen triangle is a guideline for component placement designed to provide **maximum efficiency** with the least amount of steps. Once you surpass these dimensions, you'll need to hire help! The work triangle connects the sink with the front face of the range top and refrigerator. The total of the three distances shouldn't exceed 21 feet (6.4 meters).

The most inexpensive kitchen is the most basic design incorporating standard appliances—the combination refrigerator/freezer; single unit range top with oven beneath, double sink, and dishwasher. It also makes the most efficient use of space. With more specialized equipment, the cost escalates at a rapid pace, as does the space requirement.

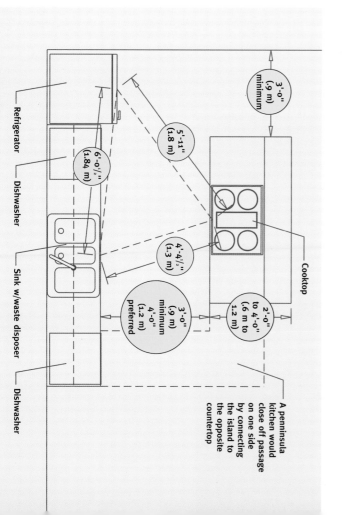

Refrigerator

Dishwasher

Sink w/waste disposer

Dishwasher

Cooktop

3'-0" (.9 m) minimum

5'-11" (1.8 m)

6'-0½" (1.84 m)

4'-4½" (1.3 m)

3'-0" (.9 m) minimum 4'-0" (1.2 m) preferred

2'-0" (.9 m) to 4'-0" (.6 m to 1.2 m)

A penninsula kitchen would close off passage on one side by connecting the island to the opposite countertop

Islands

Europeans were the first to grasp the idea of "open-concept" living with the kitchen at the core. Because living space is a precious commodity, they developed island configurations that incorporated the primary functions of preparation, cooking, and cleanup; you don't need walls to back appliances against. Sleek and minimal, freestanding units are open to positioning and allow 360-degree access, making them the consummate kitchen for casual, communal living. Storage is relegated to the perimeter.

Because they do stand on their own, islands don't have to match the surrounding cabinets. You can get some amazing character pieces at antique stores and auctions. Islands often double as table seating. The seating depth can be as shallow as 6 inches (152 mm) for just perching on stools. Islands can take any shape or form; the defining factor is that you can walk around them. The peninsula, on the other hand, is grounded at one end, trading passage for countertop and storage. Other than that, it can function the same as an island.

Screening the Mess

If you want to screen the kitchen when entertaining, look to unconventional, temporary partitions. **Doors that pocket,** have a wide swing, or slide on a barn door track, or even roll up garage style won't add much to your overall cost if incorporated during construction, but will provide flexibility. With **frosted glass or plastic inserts** in the doors, the overall impression of space will be maintained open or closed. They'll afford you the best of both worlds: an open kitchen when you're alone, a closed kitchen when you entertain.

> This beautiful loft is well suited to hosting parties. An island on wheels is easily rolled away when you need the space for large gatherings. Or, you can pull the fabric partition to hide the kitchen and create a more intimate space to gather with a few close friends.

∧ The color palette of this loft kitchen is neutral, but not boring. With charcoal walls as a backdrop, the addition of anything simple and beautifully proportioned adds fresh impact to the interior.

> Recycled stainless steel laboratory cabinets and authentic "holophane" factory lights are the focal points of this loft kitchen. The simple wood counter cantilevered over the island provides knee room. A single dry-wall corner was dropped into the loft center backing onto the dining area, thus eliminating visibility when entertaining while maintaining the open concept to the balance of the living space.

Bathrooms

Second only to the kitchen in regards to cost and first on any list of necessities is the bathroom. In the last fifty years, the bathroom has gone from a utilitarian, often communal space, to the elaborate, private spa extravaganza which incorporated everything from a gym to a juice bar, rivaling the living room in size. The new millennium has seen a more tempered approach to the bath. The fixture options are as daunting as those for the kitchen, so the choice requires some serious thought and research into what's *au courant*.

How Many Bathrooms?

The first consideration will be how many bathrooms to incorporate into your loft. This is directly related to the size of your space, and the number of people in residence.

How many people are using your bathrooms? This is a tricky question. For my loft, there are two adults in permanent residence; seldom any children, but possibly grandchildren in the future. Most of my previous generations have passed on, so designing for the elderly is low on my scale, especially since I don't intend on aging! Overnight guests are occasional but definitely a priority with me, and I do entertain, so a powder room is essential.

In a perfect world, my chart indicates a master bath with a tub for two, a steam shower, a two-sink vanity, toilet, and bidet. I would also have a powder room with sink and toilet, and a separate guest washroom with sink, toilet, tub or shower. Using the minimum and maximum specifications and fixture chart on page 69, I'll add these to my basic plan.

Your main priority should be the bathroom you use the most, generally the master bath. This is where I'm going to start. Once I have a layout that meets my approval, I can play around with options, such as adding laundry facilities in the general vicinity of the bedroom. After all, this is where most of the laundry is generated.

∧ *It's no coincidence that the revolution in bathroom design corresponded with the evolution of lofts into a sought after mode of living. The sense of airiness that deconstruction left in its wake prompted us to rebel against the dated standards and outworn conventions of the typical bathroom.*

How Many Do You Need?

I Want

	TOILET	BIDET	SINK	TUB	SHOWER	SAUNA	STEAM	VANITY
Master Bath	2	✓	2	✓	✓			✓
Main Bath	✓	1	1	for 2	✓		✓	✓
Powder Room	✓		1					

You Want

	TOILET	BIDET	SINK	TUB	SHOWER	SAUNA	STEAM	VANITY
Master Bath								
Main Bath								
Powder Room								

Plumbing

(Note: Dimensions read: width is across front, depth is front to back, and height is top to bottom of vessel.)

		MINIMUM	MAXIMUM
Toilet Standard is 2'0" wide x 2'4" deep x 2'2" high (.61 m x .71 m x .66 m).	w.	1'5" (.43 m)	2'0" (.61 m)
	d.	2'2" (.66 m)	2'7" (.79 m)
	h.	1'3" (.38 m)	7'0" (2.1 m)
Bidet Standard is 1'3" wide x 2'0" deep x 1'3" high (.38 m x .61 m x .38 m).	w.	1'2" (.36 m)	2'0" (.61 m)
	d.	2'0" (.61 m)	2'6" (.76 m)
	h.	1'2" (.36 m)	1'4" (.41 m)
Sink Standard is 1'6" wide x 1'9" long x 8" deep (.71 m x .53 m x .2 m).	w.	1'4" (.41 m)	3'2" (.97 m)
	d.	1' (.30 m)	1'10" (.56 m)
	h.	6" (1.5 m)	9" (.23 m)
Shower Standard is 3'0" wide x 3'0" deep (.91 m x .91 m).	w.	2'6" (.76 m)	no maximum
	d.	2'6" (.76 m)	no maximum
	h.	6'0" (1.8 m)	no maximum
Tub Standard is 5'0" wide x 2'6" depth x 1'6" high (1.5 m x .76 m x .46 m).	w.	5'0" (1.5 m)	6'0" (1.8 m)
	d.	2'6" (.76 m)	3'6" (1.1 m)
	h.	1'4" (.41 m)	2'0" (.61 m)

Note: Allow a minimum of 1.5" (38 mm) to an adjoining fixture, 3' (.9 m) to an adjacent wall or fixture.

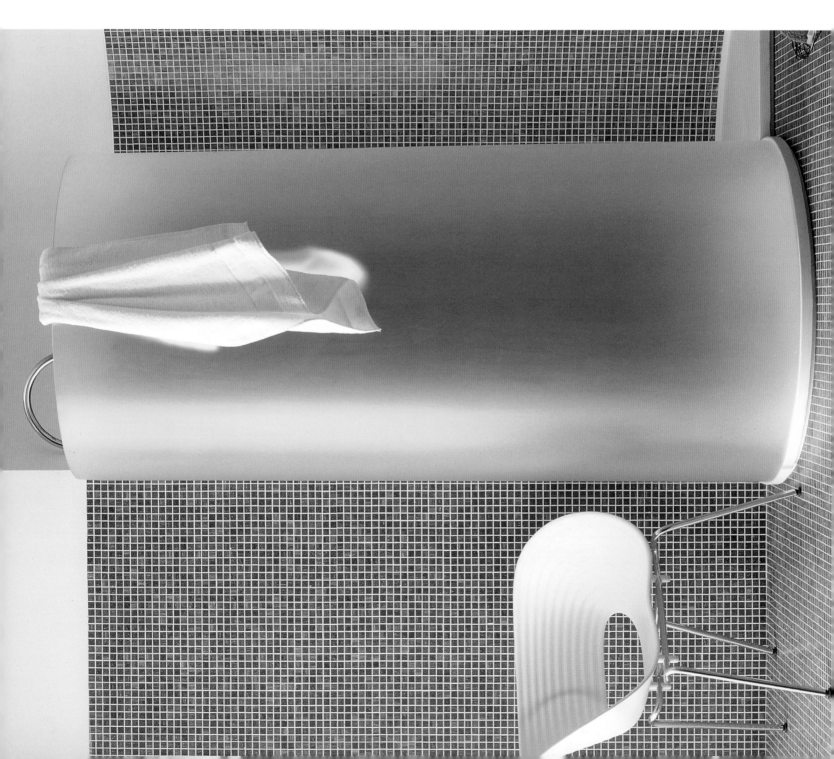

< Taking their design from the sea, Agpae's snail-shaped shower base and semicircular splash wall are a brilliant design. Glass mosaic tiles roll over curves and right angles with ease to encase the entire room; the glorious colored tiles are absolutely luminous. The contrast in scale adds to the sculptural effect of the shower.

Wet & Wild
Choosing a Shower or Bath

Do you shower, take baths, or both? I now see bathrooms with enormous showers but no tub, or vice versa. Either way, one or the other can be the focal point in the center of the room. In the case of a shower, the entire room can be tiled with a rain showerhead protruding from the ceiling and a drain in the middle of the floor.

Is your bath a solitary ablution or a social event? In other words, do you want a single tub or one designed for two or more? If you bathe daily, as opposed to showering, keep in mind how long it takes to fill a spacious tub, let alone the amount of water you'll use, and weigh that against the frequency of communal spa bathing in making your decision. Look at the water capacity of tubs you're interested in. You'll be amazed at the different volumes. In doing research for my own tub, I narrowed the field to two models similar in shape and style, both 6 feet (1.8 meters) long with one 42 inches (1067 mm) wide by 19 inches (483 mm) deep, the other 36 inches (914 mm) wide by 23 inches (584 mm) deep. I checked the amount of water required to fill them to bathing height and discovered that the 36-inch (914 mm) model required an additional 40 gallons (152 liters)! The thought of waiting impatiently every morning for the tub to fill made my decision an easy one.

One thing I've never understood is how people can purchase tubs without trying them out. To me it's the same as buying a mattress without laying on it. I know that the buoyant effect of water alters the experience somewhat, but you will find out if two people *do* fit comfortably, or if the armrests are perfect for reading, if it's long enough and if the angle of the back supports you just right. So take off your shoes and climb in with your partner if you're looking at a double tub. Disregard the confused look on the salesperson's face.

∧ The departure from an encapsulated room with wraparound fixtures hugging the walls has been fast and complete. Cube-shaped molded resin fixtures group together in the middle of this bathroom.

Bodily Functions

When marquee designers and architects like Michael Graves and Phillippe Starck entered the bathroom, nothing superfluous remained when they were through. Of course they couldn't just alter the style; when designers start something, they go all the way. **Toilets** were suspended from the wall above the floor, completing a picture of uninterrupted space when combined with a vanity similarly hung and a tub suspended in a frame, in keeping with the loft premise, and is a bonus for cleaning. Another approach makes the toilet a solid form down to the floor, freeing it from any adornment. Paired with a matching freestanding tub, they transcend space while simultaneously acting as an anchor.

Bidets were the "must have" bath fixture in the eighties, but have fallen from grace of late. Most North Americans are unfamiliar with the bidet. I once caught a gentleman using one to clean his feet! Rumor has it they were inspired by the French soldier's habit of straddling a bucket of water to wash up after a day of hard riding.

Urinals have taken over where the bidet left off. They are a great addition to any bathroom, as they are much more convenient for men to use, and they take up very little space. You can also use them as a decorative element: A home I visited for the television show *Lofty Ideas* had this marvelous cascading waterfall in the powder room. The owner used it as a backdrop to photograph models, not realizing that it was designed to be a urinal. The look on the poor man's face when I told him the intended purpose of his water feature was priceless.

< *Furniture has invaded the bathroom with fine wood vanities and framed mirrors. Add a sisal rug to keep your feet from stepping on cold tile after leaving a warm soak in the tub.*

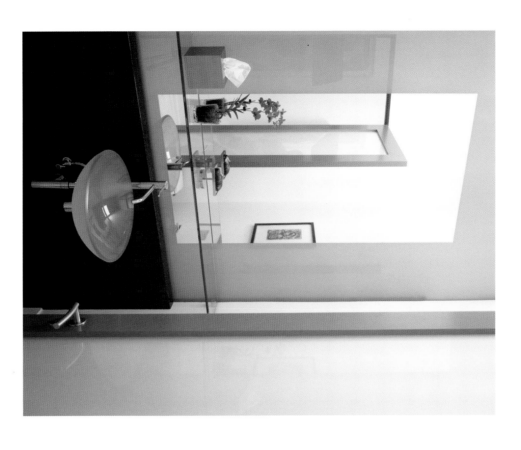

△ To maintain the sanctity of your private bathroom, a powder room is worthwhile in even the smallest of lofts. It can range from the bare minimum of a sink and toilet to multiple amenities for serving large groups at one time, or overnight guests.

While we're in the process of discussing bodily functions, what about **shaving?** I warned you that your relationship with your designer would be close. As a daily activity in your household, where does this take place—the tub, shower, or sink? If it's in the shower, allow space to sit; a built-in seat that when tiled becomes part of the architecture, a teak bench, or even a plastic stool are just a few options.

If you and your partner are both on the same schedule for work and bed, two vanity sinks would make life easier.

Hot Air

What about perks like a **sauna** or **steam room?** Both do basically the same thing, providing heat to cleanse the pores and soothe the soul. Saunas use dry heat and require a separate room lined with cedar, while a steam room can easily be installed in any enclosed shower. In both scenarios, it's important to keep your ceiling low. Hot air rises whether it's the dry heat of a sauna or wet steam, you want to be surrounded. It also takes longer to heat a larger space. A bench is welcome in either situation so you can prolong your stay. Steam can be very damaging to the rest of the room, making an airtight door and a powerful exhaust fan absolute necessities.

16 Basic Tips for Bathroom Planning

Keeping it simple is hard work. Pass up the savings at Costco for the 100 rolls of toilet paper. By the time you've driven to the 'burbs to get it, the savings are probably gone anyway. The new look whispers in a throaty voice, "restraint and elegance."

1 **Vitreous china** is a combination of clays and additives that are impervious to absorption.

2 **Porcelain-enameled steel** is an inexpensive product for lavatories and tubs. Chips to the surface are hard to repair, they're noisy, and they don't retain heat as well as other materials, but the cost makes up for these inconveniences.

3 **Cast iron** coated with porcelain enamel is also difficult to repair satisfactorily but is more resistant to chipping. It's heavy. With over-size tubs, be sure to get the weight when filled and check that your floor assembly can support it.

4 **Acrylic and ABS thermoplastics** commonly used in bathtubs are superior to polyester gel coats. They are harder, more resistant to damage and sun fading, and come in a broader range of colors.

5 It may sound silly, and you may feel silly when you do it, but do **sit on a toilet before you buy.**

6 **Look for "water conservation" toilets**—they are the socially responsible choice and some building codes demand them.

7 If possible, ask if you can see the installed toilet you're interested in and **listen to the flush.** Sound is an issue in open-concept living.

< *Rectangular troughs formed from concrete, stone, stainless steel, or wood cover the expanse previously occupied by individual sinks. Water is delivered through a delicate spout activated by hand movement.*

8 **If you want a bidet,** there are toilets available that incorporate both functions.

9 Toilets are mechanical, and like fittings, you get what you pay for. If you plan on staying in your loft, **invest in a good toilet.**

10 Be aware that **water splashes** out of a shallow sink.

11 Like kitchen sinks, **bathtubs** are measured from the widest part, not the bottom where your body actually touches.

12 **If your tub is built into a platform,** place the taps where you can reach them without falling in. The spout can go anywhere.

13 **Have a piece of plywood handy to cover the tub.** It's one of the first items installed during a renovation and contractors love to use it as a receptacle for their tools.

14 **Live with the odd blemish on antique plumbing fixtures.** Repairs never quite blend in and resurfacing makes them look like replicas.

15 **In custom showers,** include a place for soap, shampoo, etc. If you create a recessed shelf in the stud space, angle it to the front for drainage.

16 **"Open" showers** need 60 inches (1524 mm) clearance from the showerhead to adjoining fixtures if you want them to stay dry. Slope the floor to the drain.

> *Thanks to open-concept living, bathrooms have been liberated. Open to adjoining areas and outfitted with furnishings and art, they look quite at home as an extension of the living space.*

Bedrooms

The unbridled freedom of loft living has changed the way we think about the traditionally private areas. They have melded into one with the rest of the loft through partitions and doors that retract and open to expose the interior. This expands our overall perception of volume, an important trait with the shrinking size of lofts. An added bonus is always being able to enjoy the visual perspective of our public living area instead of only on weekends, when most people have time to actually sit down on that expensive sofa.

How Much Space?

The area you devote to sleeping will depend on the size of bed you choose and where your clothes are stored. When everything is organized in a walk-in closet, the room can be as small as the bed plus a passageway to get in and out. Use a standard doorway, 30 inches (762 mm), as the minimum on either side of the bed, and allow at least 36 inches (914 mm) at the bottom. This will be tight, so those partitions that open become all important. If your space lends itself more to a closet and drawers, built-ins from floor to ceiling will create a seemingly simple environment.

< Sliding doors expose sleeping quarters to the loft proper, making a small space feel bigger. The mirrored headboard, adorned with an inspirational phrase, adds to the illusion.

> Create a private sleeping area by hiding your bed behind an opaque partition wall. By leaving just enough space on either side of the bed to access your built-in storage, the open feeling of your loft can be retained.

17 Basic Tips for Bedroom Closets Storage

1 **Standard rod height** is 5'2" to 5'10" (1.6 m to 1.8 m).

2 **Get closet doors out of the way** so you can peruse everything at once.

3 **Consider pocket doors** for walk-in closets, and retractable doors that slide on a track into the closet leaving everything open, like a television cabinet for wall closets.

4 **Throw out! Give away! Store off premise**—I guarantee you'll never retrieve anything.

5 **Allow at least 3 feet** (.9 meters) for closet access.

6 **If you have opposing banks of closets,** 3 feet (.9 meters) is a must, and 4 feet (1.2 meters) is welcome. More than that is a waste, and would be better utilized inside the closet.

7 **A standard interior is 24 inches (610 mm) deep,** but by adding an extra 6 inches (152 mm), you can store shoes, ties, belts, or purses from a rack on the door. An additional 12 inches (305 mm) inside the closet and you can install shelves on the door.

8 If a **second rod** is to be installed below the main rod for shirts and jackets, locate it 3' (.9 m) above the floor.

9 For a **walk-in closet with storage on one side,** the minimum width is 5'0" (1.5 m) and the minimum depth is 5'6" (1.7 m) (not including walls, from inside to inside).

10 For a **walk-in closet with storage on both sides,** the minimum width is 7'0" (2.1 m) and the minimum depth is 5'6" (1.7 m).

11 Allow 4 to 6 lineal feet (1.2 m to 1.8 m) of **storage per person.**

12 Allow 8 to 10 lineal feet (2.4 m to 3 m) of storage for a **closet serving two people.**

13 **One foot (.3 m) of closet space** will accommodate the following items: 6 suits, 12 shirts, 8 dresses, and 6 pairs of pants.

14 Place **linen storage** near bedrooms, bathrooms, and laundry.

15 Provide a minimum of 9 square feet (.8 sq. m) storage space for a **1 to 2 bedroom dwelling.**

16 Provide a minimum of 12 square feet (1.1 sq. m) storage space for a **3 to 4 bedroom dwelling.**

17 Allow an additional 2" to 3" (51 mm to 76 mm) behind the closet rod in closets that are located at main entries for **air circulation** and additional bulkiness of overcoats.

> At one time, walk-in closets were considered the optimum in storage, but they aren't for everyone. Unless enough space is allotted, they can be claustrophobic and cluttered, defeating their purpose as an organizational device. A bank of closets lining one wall is sometimes more efficient.

Don't you just wish your closet looked like this! A place for everything and everything in its place. Spacious and open to natural light, this is the epitome of the walk-in closet.

Laundry

The last five years has seen a transformation of standard washer and dryer units. Directly related to the lifestyle changes of their markets, the bulky monsters that used to take up residence in a damp basement, or were relegated to a room of their own, have now become as streamlined as the homes they end up in. **Stackable units** were the first innovation. Designed to fit into a closet in urban townhouses and apartments, the washer and dryer are stacked on top of one another to take up less space. However, they are still deeper than a standard closet interior and leave no place for folding, sorting, or even just storing a laundry basket. Then came the **under-counter model,** my personal favorite. Front-loading rather than top-loading, and at only 24 inches (607 mm) deep, a standard counter fits over the top and it fits into a closet—addressing all the problems of laundry, except someone to do it!

Washers and Dryers Standard is 2'6" wide x 2'6"deep x 3'6"high (.76 m x .76 m x 1.1 m).

	MINIMUM	MAXIMUM
w.	2' (.61 m)	2'6" (.76 m)
d.	2' (.61 m)	3'8" (1.1 m)
h.	2'10" (.86 m)	3'6" (1 m)
Stacking washer/dryer		
w.	2' (.61 m)	2'6" (.76 m)
d.	2' (.61 m)	2'3" (.69 m)
h.	5'3" (1.6 m)	5'10" (1.8 m)

Note: Allow minimum of 3'0" (.9 m) between face of washer/dryer and wall or other obstacle. Locate laundry in close proximity to sleeping quarters.

Rack It Up!

One of the accoutrements of modern life is clothes, and lots of them. The number of clothes we have directly effects the **closet space** required. Before you determine how much space you need, I encourage you to go into your closet and drawers, removing anything you haven't worn in the last year. You don't have to part with them, just delete those peripheral items from the main equation.

Determine how many feet of hanging space you need by separating your items into full length—such as dresses, gowns, coats—and half height—for shirts, skirts, and folded pants.

Stack your sweaters to a reasonable height, three sweaters high if they're bulky, six for lightweights. How much vertical and horizontal space do they occupy? Do the same thing for other items that are stored folded, such as T-shirts, jeans, and pajamas. Take a look at what you keep in **drawers.** Is your bedroom going to have additional storage in the form of a wardrobe or chest of drawers, or do you want everything to be centralized in closets?

Line up the shoes you have out for any given season. Count the number of pairs, and then determine how much space they occupy—no one has to know the count but you! If you have boots that require a certain minimum height to stand up, account for that in your measurements and jot down the height required. Conduct the same exercise for hats, purses, belts, ties, and anything else that you store in your bedroom closets.

Finalizing the Floor Plan

The directive "measure twice, cut once," although normally used by builders, is a good mantra to use when planning a loft. The floor plan stage is essential to ending up with the space you want and the space you need. Take your time and think it through. You'll be much happier with the end result.

> I've expanded the mezzanine level so I don't have to share my closet and to reduce the ceiling height in the kitchen below for a more pleasant working environment. As an added bonus, the closet extension balances with the stairs opposite.

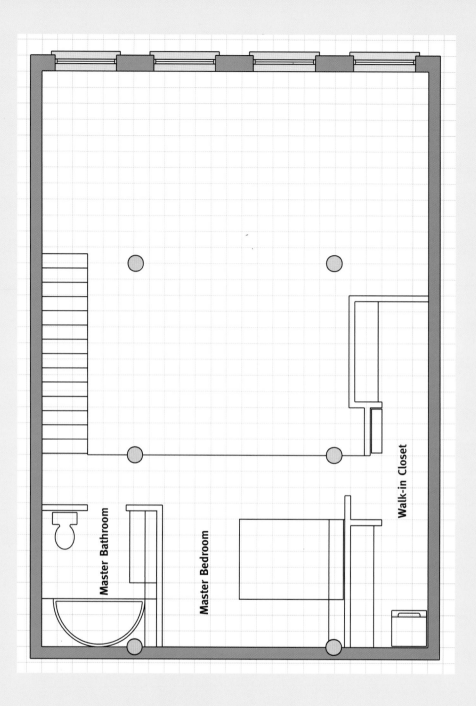

Master Bathroom

Master Bedroom

Walk-in Closet

What's Next?

With your personal needs attended to, we've covered the primary functions of your loft: sustenance, hygiene, sleep, and wardrobe. What's left of the space should be divvied up in order of priority. These will include lounging, dining, guest accommodations, and anything else your heart desires, assuming the space is available.

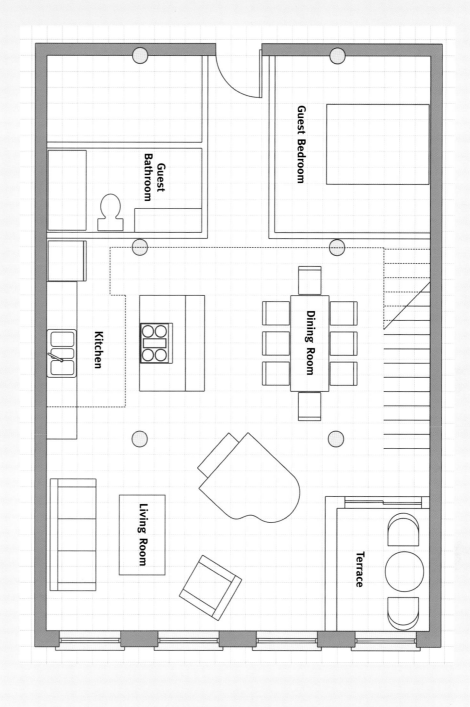

Guest Bedroom

Guest Bathroom

Kitchen

Dining Room

Living Room

Terrace

< On the main floor, the terrace was reduced to make way for a sitting area and I moved it to the opposite side where the stairs already created a corridor. I have this vision of grand volumes exploding when I enter the double height area of the loft, and a floor to ceiling long balcony enclosure across the front would have ruined the effect.

Chapter Four

Manipulating Space

Lofts, by their very nature, flaunt traditional boundaries. Manipulating space is all about carving up an open area so the passage through your loft is an adventure, an exploration that encompasses the full range of living—from gregarious party palace to intimate private zones. If you want to get a handle on this concept, throw a mattress on the floor in the center of your open loft and move in. It would be a revealing experience. I wonder how comfortable this arrangement would be?

Think about going to a discount store. Unless perfect conditions prevail—I'm not rushed, or hot, and I have comfortable shoes on—these stores make me crazy. My attention must be focused directly in front of me at close range because if I look out over the sea of never-ending merchandise crammed on racks I'll have a claustrophobic panic attack and run screaming from the store.

On the other hand, consider Barney's and Holt Renfrew. Now we're talking, and it's not just the greeter at the door, the occasional glass of champagne, or the piano player. The merchandise is often the same, starting out overpriced and ending up discount. So why can I wander aimlessly for hours at upscale stores while the discount outlets make my head spin? Because the high-end stores unwittingly entice and guide me through the experience. It is still an open expanse, but instead of having racks upon racks of indistinguishable merchandise, they arrange subtle vignettes or areas of focus with the clutter removed from sight.

< Fabric is one the oldest methods of separation: it's flexible, easily changed, and inexpensive. Voluminous draperies cascading from an impressive height add a sensuous drama to the most raw of industrial surroundings.

Creating Style with Space

Stand at the door of each location and survey the terrain. The discount store is laid out on one plane with merchandise relentlessly bombarding our vision wherever we turn. Isles are narrow; racks are packed tightly, with nothing to distract your attention from eye level. By contrast, the high-end purveyor of goods has a completely different sensibility.

Look closely at how they accomplish this clever entrapment. Sight lines are drawn up with elaborate floral displays, a sweeping staircase, or an architectural detail. We're encouraged to rest our eyes and look down at the changing vista of flooring from red to white, wood to terrazzo.

There are partition walls, but they never extend to meet the ceiling or intersect with a demising wall. Instead they punctuate the space with strong forms, grounding the expansiveness. We're lulled into complacency and the belief that not only can we afford the $500.00 pair of Manolos, but we deserve them. And isn't that the feeling everyone would like to convey in their home? These bastions of indulgence are great models for loft design because the same principles apply.

Aim for a gentle symbiosis of public and private functions when designing your loft space; separate communal areas with air instead of a wall. Challenge perspective by varying floor patterns or by elevating areas and adding a few steps. Draw the eyes up with architectural details such as a drywall partition hovering below the ceiling. Think about the flow of traffic through your loft and put up visual obstacles that let the viewer catch only a glimpse of what lies beyond, enticing them to travel the distance. Think of your loft like the human body—it's more alluring draped in a diaphanous fabric than stark naked.

Let's take a look at the basic elements you can use to designate and define the spaces in your loft.

> *Specialty stores have completely different sensibility from their discount counterparts. The space lets you breath, the layout encourages exploration and discovery.*

> As an enticement to buy, products are grouped together with a broad swathe of air left between. The intervening space defines the end of one group and the beginning of another. There are few hard edges; instead, graceful curves effortlessly propel us along at a leisurely pace.

^ The ceiling defines the functional space below by varying the height and finish materials. A composed central living core is offset on either side with energetic color and blue-collar materials, such as the rust-red steel canopy at the entrance.

Architectural Details

Architectural details are elements that are original to the building, form parts of the structure, or are decorative elements that are permanently fixed in place. They can be an integral part of the functional integrity, such as support columns or ceiling beams, air transfer ducts or plumbing pipes. Sometimes they are simply ornamental, such as a ceiling cornice or paneled wall. Assess the existing details. What elements do you like?

A freestanding colonnade of evenly spaced support columns could be the inspiration for a theme. To create a smooth functioning environment, consider these architectural anchors and how they will impact your day-to-day activities. **Columns** are imposing features; they are natural divisional elements. If they're not what you had in mind style-wise, change their look without removal—which might not even be an option for structural reasons. **Wooden posts** can be built out, round columns can be boxed and vice versa. A wide variety of **column "covers"** are sold in two halves that interlock around the existing structure.

What if your loft is devoid of architectural detail? Building methods have developed to the point where huge expanses of open space can exist without a structural column in sight. If this is the case, import your own elements. Columns are readily available in just about every conceivable material, style, size, and price range. The same applies to **cornices and decorative moldings.** These details will not only define the area, but also help develop a theme. For example, if sleek modern is your style, you can add some levity to the look with classical elements, such as Corinthian columns, or an ornate Federal style cornice decoration. Conversely, the juxtaposition of overstuffed sofas and dainty antiques against enormous concrete fluted columns provides the unexpected—synonymous with lofts.

Floors

A change in floor material is an easy way to separate areas. A tiled entrance can lead you to the **wood floor** of the body of the loft, flowing uninterrupted for a feeling of spaciousness. Two-level lofts of any size allow you the opportunity to change materials, especially if cost is a concern. Hardwood and **tile** are more costly than broadloom, so one often sees the upper level in **wall-to-wall carpet.** Most authentic lofts come with fabulous aged wood floors or **concrete**—if you are fortunate enough to have these, go with what you were blessed with and use rugs to separate functional areas.

Elevations and Planes

The action of stepping up or down conveys a feeling of **arrival and transition** from one space to another, be it from the communal hall to your private domain or the entrance to the loft proper. Even in the most modest loft, the action of changing levels makes the area feel larger. It will also vary the view by increasing sightlines on the upper level, while partially masking those below. And steps are gracious. Imagine yourself **stepping down** into a Roman bath, ready to drop the plush towel; or **stepping up** onto a dining platform in your spike-heeled Sergio Rossi pumps. (Can you tell I harbor a shoe fetish?) You can also liberate the exterior walls by raising a **central platform,** allowing the perimeter to become the passageway. No space is without a view in this scenario, and there are no redundant halls.

Which brings me to a tip on **elevations.** Always allow for a minimum of two risers. One just becomes a stumbling block.

The same sensibility can be achieved without construction—try dramatically altering the height of one object in relation to those in proximity. A vertical sculpture or vase on a console table placed behind a sofa visually separates the seating area. A tall lamp on an end table between two chairs or an armoire that functions as an entertainment unit,

freestanding between a living and dining area, will have the same effect. Reaching higher than the accompanying sofas and chairs, they break the visual perspective and define the area. Ground the space with an area rug to create a room without walls.

˄ The Fortuny light is popular in lofts for more than its crystal illumination. While the tall, slim base doesn't infringe on the floor space, those spindly legs are strong enough to support the broad umbrella head high above, subliminally reducing the gap from furnishings to ceiling.

˄ Take the Fortuny light out of the picture and the room composition is altered dramatically. In fact, there is no drama without it. The remaining furnishings and windows are all running at the same height, resulting in a mundane interior.

< The path that plumbing pipes, electrical wires, and ductwork take can map out your floor plan. Usually considered details that should be hidden behind a ceiling, many loft owners have opted for the maximum ceiling height instead of losing inches or feet boxing in huge industrial ducts.

> A dropped section can also serve as a receptacle for recessed lights that may be impossible to install if you're dealing with a concrete ceiling. For added impact, lights can also be positioned to shine up onto the original ceiling, accentuating the difference in height and finish.

Ceilings

Having satisfied your spatial needs on a horizontal plane, the vertical must also be addressed to ensure balance and comfort. The relationship between the height of the exposed ceiling and its effect on the width of the floor is a detail often overlooked.

Consider a **drywall ceiling** on one level running the length of your loft as a clean canvas to be developed. Unimpeded by furnishings, it can have the biggest impact on the overall space development, yet is often the forgotten landscape. This is especially important if the ceiling height is disproportionate to the total area. For example, a 9-foot (2.7 meter) ceiling appears lofty in a room with dimensions of 6 feet by 6 feet (1.8 meters by 1.8 meters), such as a powder room. But exposed over 40 feet by 28 feet (12.2 meters by 8.5 meters), the ceiling feels like it's sitting on your head, and if painted white, it's even more imposing. No matter what you add to the space, the white will dominate, making everything else feel cold by comparison.

Instead, break up the ceiling area. If you're dealing with a finished ceiling, add some **molding** that has a fairly substantial scale to the surface. The configuration you choose will depend on what you're defining below.

Equally efficacious in breaking up a ceiling expanse is to add a **dropped section**, particularly if you have plenty of volume. Even at a 9-foot (2.7 meter) height it can be effective, but don't drop lower than 8 feet (2.4 meters) in living areas. Dropping a finished ceiling below the original wood or concrete is dramatic by the contrast of sleek against raw. Play with what you have and endeavor to enhance it in lieu of blanket coverage with one material.

Exposed ceilings reveal the structural grid of larger beams surrounding the smaller joists. The resulting recesses can define the area below, whether they're covered with drywall or left in full view. The key is to accentuate the variances in ceiling height, creating a square or rectangular shape that will outline a functional space at floor level.

You can also take the middle road, concealing the smaller pipes and wires while leaving the larger air ducts exposed. Covered or not, these mechanical details are too big to ignore, so turn them to your advantage in defining the space. An island placed under the corrugated steel of a circular heat carrier separates the kitchen; the same duct encapsulated in a drywall box as it skims the front windows and returns into the loft on the other side creates a coffered ceiling outlining the living room below.

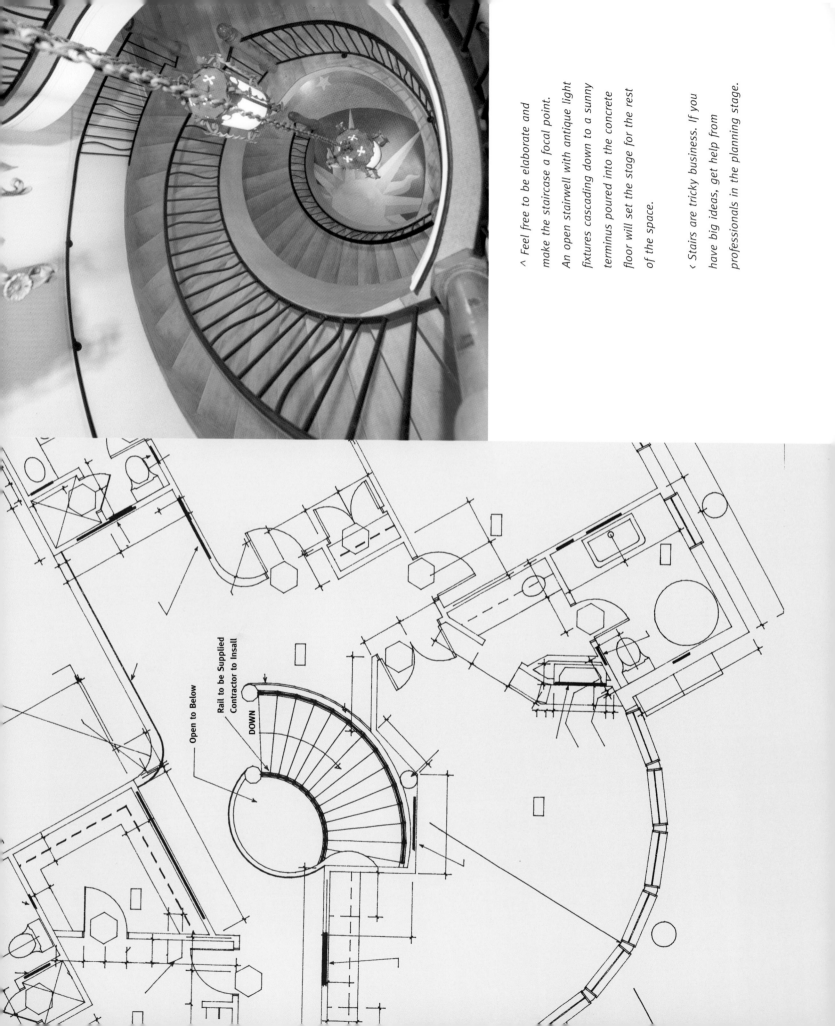

∧ Feel free to be elaborate and make the staircase a focal point. An open stairwell with antique light fixtures cascading down to a sunny terminus poured into the concrete floor will set the stage for the rest of the space.

< Stairs are tricky business. If you have big ideas, get help from professionals in the planning stage.

Open to Below

Rail to be Supplied Contractor to Insall

DOWN

Staircases

On equal ground with columns, staircases are a prominent architectural feature that, by their scale, can manipulate the loft into manageable areas without the use of conventional walls. Rigged like yachts with halyards, turnbuckles, and cables, or traditional in styling with carved newel posts and pickets, they will become an integral part of the overall design.

Adding a Second Floor

Keep in mind that vaulting ceilings are one of the defining features of a loft, so when adding a second floor, make sure that a portion of the full height is retained. Consider the use of the space below the second floor. Vast, empty voids above our heads are not always conducive; candlelight dining will feel more intimate in a confined area whereas volumes of air space seemingly expand the floor area when it's wall to wall people at a party. Kitchens are often relegated to a lower ceiling height. With an island set within the kitchen but beyond the dropped ceiling, you achieve the best of both. Bathrooms are another area where a lower ceiling is often desirable.

If the second level is small, you may want to use it as a sitting room or home office. Most commonly, we find the master bedroom suite located at the top of the loft. It's the perfect vantage point to survey your accomplishment, however, it's the hottest spot in the loft (hot air rises), and then there are those stairs to maneuver every night—remember it's your personal space, so tailor it to suit your needs.

> A stunning cast iron window separates functions in this loft. Its central position allows it to be enjoyed and appreciated from more than one vantage point.

Windows

Windows are another architectural detail that can help define your area without putting up walls. If your windows are scattered throughout, anything grouped around them will have its own demarcation. Typically in old warehouses, the windows ran consecutively around the perimeter. Windows that relate to different areas can be distinguished by their window dressings, even if the treatment is just for show. A living room positioned centrally in front of a perimeter wall can be defined by full length drapes that border the windows on the outside of the grouping, with the adjoining windows left unadorned, or covered with a different treatment. The full height drapes needn't be operable, but their presence is a bold outline.

Reclamation

Salvage yards and auction sales of old buildings, both residential and commercial, can yield some exciting materials. Reclaimed architectural details like **tin ceilings, columns,** resplendent **arched windows or doors** come "as is," requiring your floor plan to adhere to their dimensions, which consequently impacts the segmentation of the space. The effort involved is inconsequential if you come across a piece of antiquity worth salvation but it does take some finessing. To fit the scale of lofts, commercial salvage is often most fruitful.

In one Manhattan loft, the master bath was entirely clad in slabs of Carrera marble—floor, ceiling, magnificent Roman tub, as well as a separate shower resplendent with an elaborate brass rail surround. This bathroom had been the private domain of a bank president; it was adjacent to his office at the bank's headquarters. One of our clients was blessed to be in the right place at the right time. He bought "the room" complete with solid brass fittings *and* porcelain toilet, all the marble, and a piece of New York history, which is priceless. The new bathroom was sized to fit the reclaimed materials in the planning stage.

Air Space

Maximize the potential of the space available. Show it off by resisting the temptation to fill every nook and cranny. Loft design by necessity can become an exercise in editing, where we pare down the possessions of a conventional home to fit into an open exposure environment. In cities where square foot costs have skyrocketed, the biggest testament to your success is a "wide open spaces" sensibility where each setting has room to breathe and stimulate the senses.

When designing your loft, leave open space for people instead of isolating rooms and cramming them with furnishings. Take advantage of lockers to store redundant pieces. Realtors should adjust their valuation tables to reflect elbow room over room count! With wall space at a premium, you'll appreciate your art collection more if each piece is prominently placed and enjoyed, then exchanged for another when you're ready for a new perspective.

> A loft's most attractive feature is its space. Don't feel the need to place to much furniture or art into it. By being selective about the furnishings and their placement, you'll be embracing the open-feeling appeal and fostering a healthy, enticing living area.

Partitions

Even if your loft demands definitive separation, there are alternatives to typical wall assemblies. Low partition walls that rest below the ceiling will give you visual privacy and reduce a vast ceiling height to a more human scale while still maintaining that lofty appeal.

If sound is an issue, consider installing a **glass transom** to join the drywall to the ceiling. A continuous run of clear glass will virtually disappear, affording you the benefit of sound attenuation and visual appeal.

The bathroom may be the only area you need to encapsulate with a ceiling to house exhaust fans and capture sound. In a smaller loft, drop the ceiling over the partition walls rather than utilizing the actual ceiling of the loft for unimpeded ceiling lines. To create an illusion of height inside the bathroom, cap the ceiling with **Plexiglas** and exhaust through the walls. In an expansive loft where your ceiling doesn't need any illusions to make it appear higher, consider building that one room up the full height. The room could become an amazing feature, akin to structural columns.

< Try not to think only in terms of conventional sheetrock walls for separations. There are so many creative options available that will afford separation without boxing you in. An ingenious photographer suspended his work from the ceiling pipes with chain to facilitate a gallery for clients and a screen for the private areas of his loft.

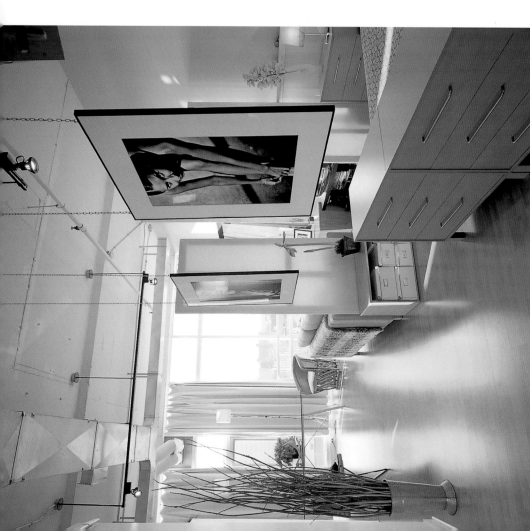

Fabric

Consider alternatives that allow you to use the space in different ways. A drywall partition is fixed, unless it's constructed as freestanding on wheels, which is an option. Traditional **draperies** are economical and practical, offering ease of operation and installation. **Flat panels** operate on the same premise but with a more tailored appearance. What they lack in dramatic volume is made up for with **translucency** that allows you to glimpse what lies beyond, especially when properly illuminated. Made from fabric or tightly woven glass fiber mesh, they can slide on tracks to expose or screen.

Look to your surroundings for inspiration. A Vancouver loft owner who had a view of the sailboats in the harbor devised partitions from sailcloth that operated on a block-and-tackle system using marine hardware to open or close access to the bedroom.

I've noticed the booths at trade shows I attend are constructed of stretchy, lightweight fabrics pulled taut over a frame. The configurations can be spectacular, limited only by the frame's shape. What do you get when you combine two hula-hoops and a length of fabric that falls floor to ceiling with a pocket sewn at the top and bottom? A pretty groovy column. Add a light inside and you've got your own spectacle.

< The inherent translucence of fabrics allows the penetration of diffused light as well as requisite privacy. The barely visible geometrical grid of the frame beneath is a subtly erotic touch.

^ For a simple, fixed partition, sew canvas into a large pocket and slide it over an artist's stretcher frame.

Glass

If you're lucky enough to have an exterior vista like a movie backdrop, you won't want to obstruct the view. There are myriad products available that make it possible to maintain the flow of natural light while still declaring intimate areas. An **interior glass wall** is the obvious first choice. Clear panels can provide optional privacy with the installation of curtains, sandblasting will obscure the view, or films can be applied that allow for one way or certain angle viewing—quite a unique effect.

While expensive, glass is an easy-to-maintain, versatile material. **Tempered glass** can be used for walls, doors, kitchen counters, and bathroom sinks. **Glass blocks** have "been around the block" so to speak, and they're still popular in lofts for their versatile configurations and patterns that run the gamut from clear to fully obscured with every possibility in between.

Plastic

Inexpensive, lightweight, self-supporting, and easy to install, plastic products have come in from the cold in the guise of walls, doors, columns, dropped ceilings, shower enclosures, and illumination covers.

Polycarbonate sheets designed for greenhouse coverings comprise two sheets of plastic separated by an air space. While offering up to 83 percent light transmission in its clear form, the tinted, triple wall version transmits almost the same light, but the refraction obscures the view to the other side making it ideal in a bedroom or bath situation.

Acrylic-modified panels, originally designed for exterior signage, share the same characteristics plus a few extra design features such as embedded metal and crystal.

< Handmade paper sandwiched between clear glass panels has the sereneness of a shoji screen without the delicate temperament.

Reinforced fiberglass panels made with pure acrylic resin display a web of silken threads that softly diffuses transmitted light. Tinted, pigmented, translucent, or opaque are also available. You can even get the bullet-resistant acrylic panels if your neighborhood is still in transition!

v Doors and transoms fabricated of thermal plastic not only allow the transmission of light but also carry less visual weight than their wood or steel counterparts. The panels can be mounted onto steel drywall studs, framed with drywall edging, or inserted in a custom metal frame.

> Make doors as tall as possible, especially if the partition connects with the ceiling. Such a simple change instills the illusion of height and establishes a strong character.

∨ Back-to-back showers are separated with a plastic panel manufactured for use in signage. Natural light is shared between the two separate bathrooms.

Screens

Screening an area, such as the bedroom, can be seductive. The **steel mesh** used to make protective fireplace screens is almost surreal in it's allure when cascading from a high-ceilinged loft or suspended below rafters, and prompts us to remember the building's origins when installed in a sleek interior. The best part is that it can run on a track allowing you to remove the barrier at your discretion.

Lattice associated with landscape design can produce a similar effect, especially when made of 1-inch by ¼-inch (25 mm by 6.4 mm) stock molding in a grid pattern. The closer you position the molding, the more streamlined the silhouette, and the shadows thrown from the passage of light are amazing. If you're really ambitious, weave pliable lath, strips of **wood veneer,** or **leather** through the openings.

∧ Chain mail, ironically enough, has the softest feel and hangs like luxurious drapery. Only the light from a lamp gives any indication of the bedroom on the raised platform beyond.

Drywall

Drywall partitions (also known as sheetrock, gypsum board, and wallboard) are the most common and least expensive method of acquiring privacy, but they don't have to be mundane. Panels interjected with a well-judged cutout will emit shafts of light from the space beyond. Curve walls to gently nudge traffic through. Make the doors as tall as possible, especially if the partition connects with the ceiling. Such a simple change adds elegance, permanence, class, and a feeling of stability.

Doors can be installed simply as a framework for outstanding doors. Barn doors have become associated more with lofts than barns these days. They allow you to pick the material and finish for the impending door, be it wood or metal, and the width of the area you wish to reveal. An entire room can be exposed when you think of how wide barn openings are. Look for smoothly operating tracks from commercial door manufacturers.

Doors

Wide swinging or **pocket doors** installed below the ceiling provide privacy without chopping up and foreshortening the space. Installed with opaque glass or plastic windows, the room beyond remains an integral part of the loft whether open or closed and allows the transfer of light, particularly important in long lofts with windows at only one end. The operating hardware is critical; there is nothing worse than having to remove a wall because a pocket door came off it's track. Piano hinges will allow the door to fold back flat onto the wall. Before ordering door pulls, confirm the dimensions will fit the depth of your door. Most European hardware has smaller escutcheon plates (the ring that covers the hole) making it necessary to order doors without predrilled holes. Have a qualified installer hang the doors; it's a real art, particularly in old buildings with uneven floors.

Storage

Storage solutions can serve several purposes. A drywall monolith that houses the refrigerator on one side, enclosed storage on the other, and an office above, can anchor the center of a loft and separate functional spaces while leaving the ceiling unscathed.

Storage can double as a partition. Open shelves will create partial visibility; add industrial wheels, and it can be moved to suit the occasion. Keep in mind that once filled with books or clothes the mobility of a wheeled unit may be considerably diminished.

< *A full partition wall transforms the same loft into a conventional condominium.*

> *A double-sided fireplace maximizes the potential of the space available. Sharing warmth with the elevated bedroom beyond, the narrow wall connecting the chimney to the ceiling also creates an intimate environment with an air of exclusivity.*

∧ *The exposed area under the mezzanine showcases the loft's generous proportions.*

Fireplaces

There is something mesmerizing about fireplaces, and nothing is more welcoming. It must hearken back to the romantic notion of hearth and home. Because of ventilation innovations in gas fireplaces, they can be installed almost anywhere. Connected to the exterior by a low partition wall, a two-sided fireplace positioned high on one side and at floor level on the elevation side can be an ingenious separation. The partial wall provides storage, separation, and on the elevated side, privacy where only the head of the occupant will be visible with three or four risers up. The fireplace face on the floor level side will be visible from afar due to its high position on the partition wall, making it a design element to be enjoyed in more than one location.

For those on the top floor of a loft building, a centrally located fireplace with a stack rising to the ceiling will have as much prominence and separation value as an elaborate staircase.

> An understated and rather austere hallway removed from natural light is animated with narrow translucent doors. The heavy framed mirror resting on the floor foreshortens the corridor and anchors the space with its strong color.

Wall Finishes

Color and texture can transcend physical limitations when applied to wall surfaces. Functional spaces can acquire their own identity when designated by a distinctive wall finish or a change in texture, say from neutral white walls to a corner in gloss red to indicate the dining room. A less dramatic but equally effective transition can be the subtle textural change from flat drywall to rough, scratch-coat plaster that's conventionally used as an undercoat.

Take some cues from set designers who have long been accustomed to creating illusions. If you are strapped with a long hall, try diminishing the width at one end, which will create a vanishing point. You can accomplish this successfully without construction simply by painting one wall darker than the other, even if you stick to light colors, such as white on one side and tan on the opposite. The result will be like railroad tracks appearing to narrow as they distance themselves.

Adding an Edge

Transforming an empty space into a personal home affords limitless possibilities. Take your time and explore some options during the design process. If the architecture of your loft is unremarkable, choose not to acknowledge it. Instead, shift the orientation of the loft from the right angles as defined by the party walls to the diagonal. You can do this by simply rearranging the furniture. This unorthodox application will add an unparalleled edginess and a definite sense of movement. Visitors will be unable to discern the original shape of the space.

Play with your loft even if you're unable to make any substantial physical alterations. Create illusions using perspective and the shadows of directional lighting. These techniques will not only bring the loft to life, they will help make a large space seem more intimate and a small space more open.

Your personal living requirements may demand closed areas, particularly if you work from home. Break up a long corridor of multiple openings by angling one wall, or stagger the walls and conceal the door openings into the setbacks.

< Angled walls and bold color differentiate areas in this unconventional loft. Partition walls float below the ceiling to communicate the overall size, with the structural columns acting as reference points.

∧ When styling your loft, combine strains of classical concepts mixed with modernity (or vice versa) to provide an enduring look. A French armoire and the galleried photographic images impart energy to this somberly handsome interior.

Chapter Five

Style

Architect Louis Sullivan is credited with the famous adage "form follows function." Simply put, design and composition should be determined by the purpose of a thing. Our floor plan to this point reflects what the functions of the loft are; now we will determine the form—the style.

Viewed as the fun part of design, this is often the most difficult exercise even for professionals when we're doing our own homes. There are just so many options out there—almost too many! Some people are lucky enough to be very specific in their likes and dislikes; but most, like myself, covet more than one style. So many diverse genres hold infinite appeal that it's hard to settle on one "look," a penchant I once considered a downfall, but now appreciate as an attribute. A mix of styles far surpasses a strict design mantra in terms of longevity, and yields a richly layered look. It can act to offset a worn industrial setting, and is easier to alter when you want to bring new life into the space, because you are not limited to a specific style.

Keep in mind that subdued and subtle illusions will provide a design that is more malleable to our changing taste. Instead of reconstructing the Medici Palace inside your loft, allude to Italian style. An arcade composed of a number of arches in an amorphous living area, rough plaster walls in a personal space, or a tiled vanity with an iron base in a bathroom will give you an Italian feeling without being blunt.

A large-scale treatment doesn't require reinforcement with every other addition to the room. Interiors that are a mixture of showcased concepts are more inviting and comfortable because of their diversity. You won't feel like you're living in a museum or Disney World.

Historical representation can plunge you into the same design cesspool. Instead of filling your loft with archi-tectural details, furnishings, art, and accessories depicting a particular era, a combination of period paint colors on the walls, an antique armoire, or Oriental carpets can bring Old World elegance to a raw interior.

What's Your Style?

Where do you look to find your personal style? Take inspiration from the things that interest you—magazines, movies, books, theater, television, galleries, travel, or nature. Tear pages from magazines that have appealing room settings and keep them in a file. Movies are also a great source for design ideas, and you can actually see how people live in the settings. Visit furniture, antique, and salvage stores armed with a camera. Don't forget museums and galleries. When you've exhausted all possibilities, study your collection. The majority of clients who walk into our office adamantly claim they have no design preferences but when confronted with examples of different interiors, they are invariably drawn to a particular style. Examine your choices to determine what drew you to that interior. Was it the color, the furniture, the paintings, the pairing of elements? Once you've established your personal taste, the rest is easy.

Take your time and cull resources for items that meet your design mandate. Refer to your file clippings regularly through the renovation process and keep pertinent examples with you on your shopping expeditions so you aren't tempted to stray too far from your design objective.

< Travel is a strong motivator—we all want reminders of a fond vacation. The tasteful representation of an Asian motif showcases a handcrafted dining table and artful seating as opposed to dragons and paper lanterns.

> The sectional sofa flanked by an end table fabricated from an ancient salvaged beam and a worn leather club chair exemplifies adoption of complementary but contrasting materials. Composed of upholstered single mattresses, the sofa doubles as beds for overnight guests.

Tricks of the Trade

There are several basic principles of design that may or may not apply to your particular situation; it's not necessary to adopt every one. The key is to envision your home and what you put into it, keeping in mind the principles that apply to your specific loft, and you'll make fewer returns on unsuitable items.

Balance

Balance is what gives design stability. Typically, we think of balance as "matching," such as columns flanking both sides of a door or a sofa with end tables and lamps on both sides. The objects are of equal weight and form, equidistant from a central axis; this evokes a formal, calm attitude. There's nothing wrong with that, but too much balance of this nature can lead to boredom. There are actually two kinds of balance: **symmetrical** (as described above) and **asymmetrical**, which is a little more difficult to achieve but important for its more casual, dynamic aesthetic.

To create an asymmetrically balanced arrangement, place different objects at unequal distances from a central axis; ideally, the objects will be counterbalanced. Conversely, disparate forms with the same apparent visual mass can balance each other when placed equidistant from a central axis. Envision your space with everything placed in matching pairs—feels pretty stiff doesn't it? Now look again, replacing half the symmetrical items with those that counterbalance instead of balance, or match. Much more interesting, isn't it? This is hard to grasp, and even more difficult to accomplish. Ask my girlfriend. Whenever we shop for one of her many homes, she's always matching; I'm always saying, "No, we don't want it to match." This debate has gone on for years.

∧ Pedigreed furnishings, strict contours, and intricate wall patterns negate the need for superfluous accessories. Replicating the geometric pattern on the walls, ceilings, and the floor subtly encapsulates the room in austere serenity.

> Edgy and dynamic, this setting has wonderful appeal. The symmetry is obvious: the parallel arrangement of stacked storage to the bench/coffee table. More subliminal is the asymmetric value: the long, red suspended cabinet counterbalanced by the bulkier red floor model and offset chair.

Rhythm

Rhythm is described as "an ordered recurrent alternation of strong and weak elements" according to *Webster's* dictionary. It invigorates with diversity while repetition connects disparate parts. Consider the flow of a song. A particular sequence of notes forms the basis of the composition and they are played loud and soft, verbally and instrumentally, start to finish. The only significant change is what they refer to as "the break," which is a complete departure from the original pattern. This is thrown in to keep the song from becoming boring and staid. I've read that the Beatles often used this device—when John Lennon wrote a song, Paul McCartney did the break and vice versa, just to keep the music edgy.

Rhythm and repetition go hand-in-hand in design as well as music. In good interiors, you won't even make the connection, you'll just feel it—comfortable yet keen. The rhythm and subsequent repetition are almost subliminal. **Patterns** can be developed using **shape, size, color,** or **material** mimicked throughout the space, thus creating the rhythm. A freestanding vertical enclosure to house a refrigerator or pantry can be repeated elsewhere to function as a closet.

You don't have to replicate patterns exactly. For example, the curvaceous lines of a partition wall designating the entrance can reappear on the kitchen island and living area sofa; the areas in between form the "break."

The mass of a built-in home entertainment center can be mirrored in the kitchen cabinetry. A color introduced at the entrance can be reinforced through a painting and throw cushions on a sofa in other areas of the loft. You can create a sequential change by repeating several shades of one color at chosen intervals. The eye will barely perceive the change, but the senses will be acutely aware. Don't feel you have to pick one detail to develop. Two or more patterns repeated alternately or as progressive units can create a dynamic rhythm.

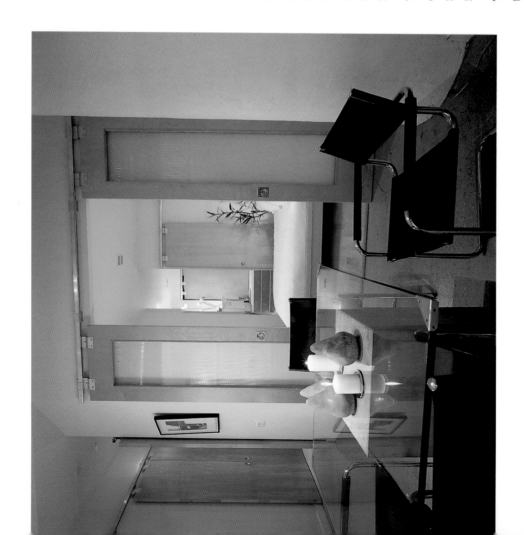

˄ *The size of this loft is accentuated by a progression of doors that open to reveal the interior. Finished with the same wood, their imposing rectangular shape and staggered installation forms a rhythmic composition.*

Emphasis

If you think of your loft as a picture, you will understand that it needs a focal point and this is where emphasis comes in. Don't rush to an art gallery to purchase an enormous, eye-catching painting. Not only the unique commands attention. Unusual relationships between objects of size, color, or texture can do this just as well. Think of a grand piano, a red wall, or a circular table in the middle of a large entry hall with nothing competing with its presence. The prerequisite for emphasis is contrast. And never underestimate the power of uninterrupted air—in a crowded room nothing commands more attention.

Creating a Focal Point

Designer Syrie Maugham was famous for her all white rooms, and I'm talking everything from the floor to the furnishings. How did she create emphasis? She filled a room with small-scale pieces set close together, except for the focal point—that was set off on its own, was in a larger scale or texture, and illuminated to set it apart. Had she added a single red flower, our eyes would have been riveted to that one small element because the **contrast** would have been so shocking. By the same token, a plethora of sleek, shiny surface materials will play second fiddle with the introduction of a singular, richly textured matte object just because the difference will be so noticeable.

Nothing works better than **lighting** to elevate even the most mundane of items to a prominent focal point. In a room illuminated with incandescent lamps, the clear white light that emanates from a tiny halogen spotlight will set the object apart by the dissimilarity, not only of color, but also of beam spread. Traditional light bulbs emit a dull, yellow glow that softly washes over an area, whereas halogen bulbs transmit bril-

liant white light that encompass a distinctly smaller range with a sharp cut-off that frames the object under illumination. The fixture can be ceiling mounted or a freestanding unit with an adjustable head that can be set to focus in on an object for the desired effect. Of all the elements involved in creating emphasis, lighting is the most important.

Limit the number of dominant items you fit into the space. Too many conflicting elements can lead to a very unsettling venue. Modern design characterized by strong architectural forms and neutral color schemes rely on a hit of color through art—**a change of texture,** possibly introduced with a bleached deep shag cotton carpet, or a grandiose, antique wooden sideboard with a soft patina to bring it warmth. A loft filled with Old World antiques is set apart by the abstract paintings adorning the walls. Exaggerate and simplify, mix and match, overdo and underplay disparate pieces of visual culture to create a testimony to your lifestyle. Remember—one person's idea of "clean" leaves another cold!

> A fabulous view of the city captures all our attention when accompanying furnishings are kept simple. Unencumbered by draperies and accentuated with mirrors, day or night, it's magnificent.

Furnishings

Before the floor plan can be finalized, the furnishings need to be put into place. When we design for a client, we draw in basic furniture sizes, then source out the exact items we want, making alterations to the plan based on our findings. Sometimes we'll come across a fabulous piece that we've just got to have and it may be very unique dimensionally, so I advise selecting everything before finalizing the plan. Avoid the technical glitch of allowing space for a king-size bed and then purchasing a regal bedstead that adds considerably to the overall dimension. You may find, as I do, that the items you're drawn to provide inspiration for not only the style of your loft, but also the physical layout. An incredible mirror that demands a commanding location also needs a wall to lean on. A to-die-for antique sideboard may require a knee-wall where none was called for.

Work through the occasional setbacks when you introduce a new piece you just had to have, but are disappointed with once you get it home. Don't despair. Live with it for a while and a resolution will come to you. Often the addition or removal of items you're not as attracted to will remedy the situation. Tantamount to the enjoyment of your loft is comfort; never sacrifice it for aesthetic. They should go hand-in-hand.

Open-concept lofts of municipal proportions work best when furnishings are arranged in convivial groupings grounded by area rugs that define their boundaries. Carefully place furnishings to create passageways that direct you through the loft without a wall in sight. An intimate library arrangement of bookshelves and chairs can denote a transition to the more private bedroom. Avoid lining everything up the same way, which creates a "dormitory" look—not a quality you would usually want associated with your home. Whatever your preferences, try and develop fluid arrangements that flow one into the other.

< Comingle blue chip furnishings with flea market. Canvas scroll panels focus our attention on the exotic wood headboard that doubles as a storage unit. The salvaged cooler is a supplemental repository and a nod to the building's roots.

Standard Sizes for Common Furniture Pieces

FURNITURE		STANDARD SIZE
Lounge chair		3' w x 3' d (.91 m x .91 m)
Sofa		7' w x 3' d (2.13 m x .91 m)
Sofa bed	(extended)	7' w x 6'6" d (2.13 m x 1.98 m)
Loveseat		6' w x 3' d (1.82 m x .91 m)
Chaise		2'6" w x 6'1" (.76 m x 1.85 m)
Coffee tables	rectangle	3'6" w x 2'd (1.06 m x .60 m)
	square	3'6" w x 3'6" d (1.06 m x 1.06 m)
	round	3'6" diameter (1.06 m)
End tables	rectangle	2'3" w x 1'10"d (68 m x .55 m)
	square	2' w x 2' d (.60 m x .60 m)
	round	2'4" diameter (.71 m)
Console tables		6' w x 1'4" d (1.82 m x .40m)
Dining tables	rectangle	3'6" w x 6' d (1.06 m x 1.82 m)
	square	4' w x 4' d (1.21 m x 1.21 m)
	round	4' diameter (1.21 m)
Barstool		1'6" w x 1'8" d (.45 m x .50 m)
Dining chair		1'6" w x 1'8" d (.45 m x .50 m)
Arm chair		2' w x 1'8" d (.60 m x .50 m)
Mattress	Single	3'3" w x 6'3" (.99 m x 1.90 m)
	Double	4'6" w x 6'3" d (1.37 m x 1.90 m)
	Queen	5' w x 6'8" d (1.52 m x 2.03 m)
	King	6' w x 7' d (1.82 m 2.13 m)
	California king	6'4" x 6'8" (1.93 m x 2.03 m)
	Add 3" to 6" (.07 m to .15 m) width and 6" to 12" (.15 m to .30 m) with headboard and footboard.	
Night table		2'2" w x 1'7" d x 2'4" h (.66 m x .48 m x .71 m)

Lines

We're affected by everything we're exposed to, if only subconsciously. The mix of lines that comprise your furniture will reflect on your personality and impart a definite feeling in the room. **Horizontal or straight lines** are restful, positive, and direct while **vertical lines** embody strength and dignity—definite musts in any composition. **Curved lines** are gentle, passive, and elegant—a pleasant interjection.

Think about what you want to focus on in the loft. Stately Corinthian columns, the ones with the wedding cake top, won't fight for prominence if they're offset with sleek furnishings of a common low height. In this scenario, the furnishings provide the horizontal line attributes, the columns dignity and elegance with their vertical height and curves.

< A loft devoid of architectural details can still incorporate lineal structure. Standing out against a charcoal backdrop, minimalist wall cabinetry is offset by the conical light sculpture and rectangular fireplace wall for a balanced visage.

Storage in Furniture

The consumerism of our society always brings us back to a quest for storage. You would think that when presented with volumes of open space we'd be able to designate a percentage to storage. But space is a precious commodity, making it difficult to relegate to mundane functions. Prune your possessions in the same way you clean out your closet. Be diligent. Take the opportunity of moving to literally *clean house* of redundant, outdated, or just plain distasteful items—even if it was a gift from your best friend! Utilize the storage locker that came with your loft to store excess baggage: put superfluous art and accessories on a rotation and rid your living space of seasonal paraphernalia.

Interior perimeter walls are the easiest to sacrifice, solving the two-fold dilemma of essential storage and surface finish for a vast expanse of demising material. Located under a mezzanine, a bank of cabinets built floor to ceiling and wall-to-wall when construction is underway is an inexpensive solution. Designed to resemble retail "bunks" with open cubes of identical size, the unit can house everything from audio/visual equipment to books and collectibles.

> A storage unit that exerts pressure on the ceiling of a traditional residence will help to compress the height in an industrial loft. Large-scale paintings hung low on the wall and pendant lights dropping from the ceiling all improve the relationship between the floor and ceiling, enhancing the enjoyment of the space.

An asymmetric pattern of shelves requires more detailed planning. Unless you're a meticulous purist, the addition of doors provide an opportunity for concealment and can convert mayhem into harmony. Disguised completely with concealed hardware, the outline of each door will be the only clue to the existence of what lies behind and the linear pattern will provide a subtle graphic wall treatment.

Freestanding storage units can double as partitions. Watch the proportions between the ceiling height and surrounding furnishings. A towering shelving system below a double-height ceiling may seem appropriate, but next to a low profile seating or sleeping arrangement, it will feel like it's about to fall on you! Save the really high pieces for outside walls. Once strictly the domain of libraries, rolling ladders have made a comeback with the advent of lofts, making the upper extremities accessible.

> The choice of cladding material will have a tremendous impact—glossy materials, deep hues, illuminated obscure panels, and bold figured wood will grab your attention. A matte, discreet finish that matches the adjoining vertical surface will make the unit disappear into the background.

< Banish that picture of the boring wall unit—stainless steel, cast iron, exotic woods, and new operating hardware have transformed storage to sculpture.

Adding Style to Your Floor Plan

Deciding where everything goes and the amount of space each area needs is only the first part of the plan. Stage two consists of adding style and making it your own. Adding the details to your floor plan can really make your loft come alive.

My Final Floor Plan, Mezzanine

The mezzanine has grown again. Looking from the window wall in, the extension is much more interesting than the old straight line and will act as a buffer to the bed. What a great spot to lounge on a chaise and appreciate my domain!

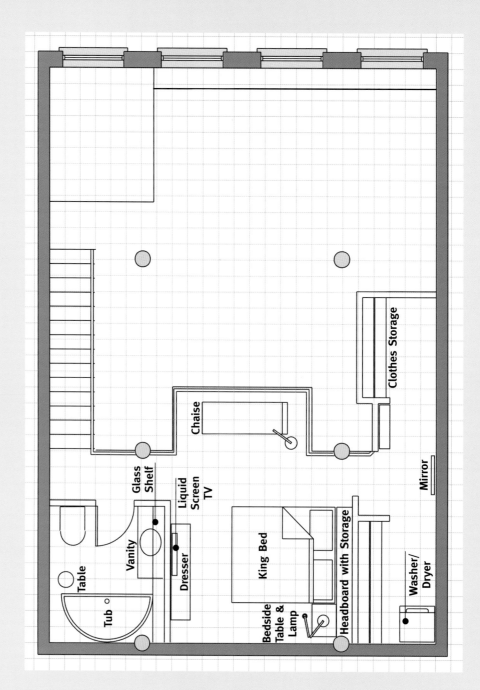

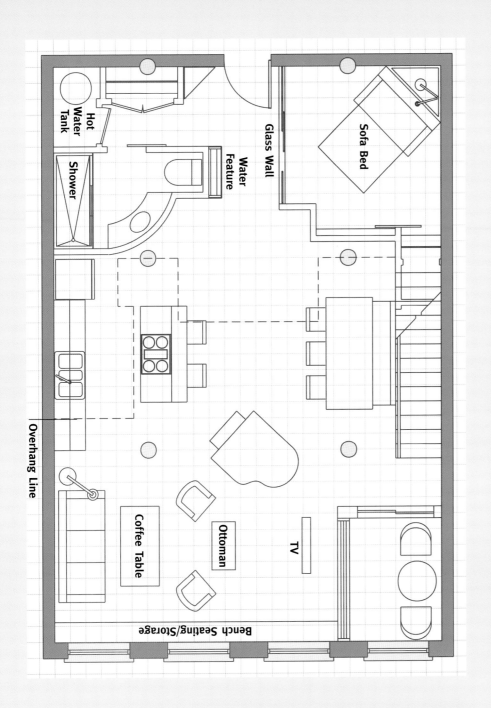

Hot
Water
Tank

Shower

Glass Wall

Water
Feature

Sofa Bed

Overhang Line

Coffee Table

Ottoman

TV

Bench Seating/Storage

My Final Floor Plan, Main Floor

I've squeezed the entrance so the body of the loft will appear vast by comparison. To ward off oppression, the guest wall has been glazed and a water feature incorporated opposite. The walls have been stepped and curved for more interest and to accentuate the columns in front. Moving the piano further from the window wall to make room for additional seating infringed on the dining space, resulting in replacement of the chairs on one side for bench seating. The Domino effect.

Or, I Could...

...Leave the loft at one level. The piano would have to go and windows would have to be the extent of my fresh air access, but overall, I could be quite happy living here.

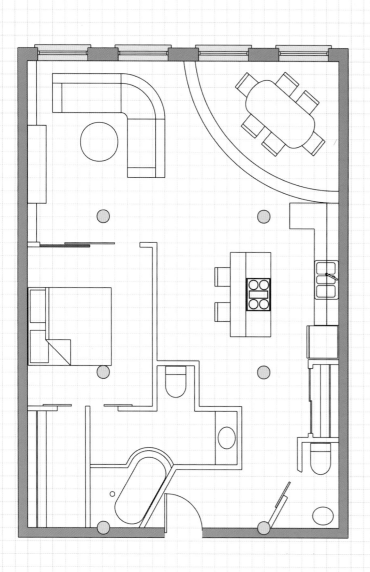

...Lose the terrace. The seating area in front of the windows could be elevated making the physical space much more provocative. I quite like this one.

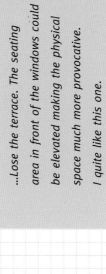
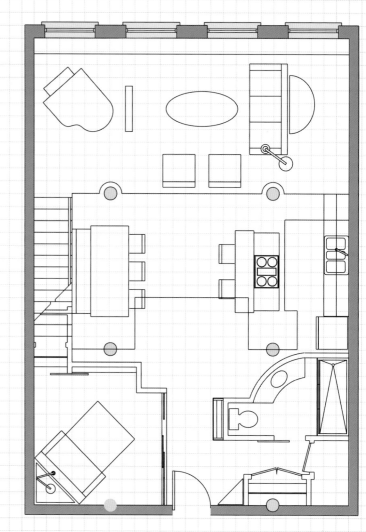

...Remove the piano thereby fulfilling my wish to seat twenty for dinner if I jockey the other furniture around. Definitely my least favorite.

...Dispose of the guest room and add back what is important to my daily life. Elevating the living area by two risers reduces the stairway to the upper level. It also reduces the number of steps required to reach the upper level. Except for the door opening directly into the dining room, this one is pretty good too.

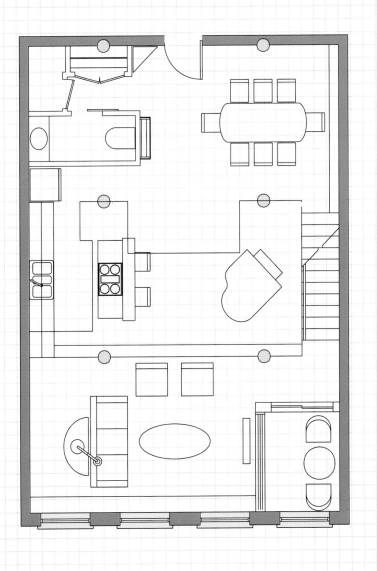

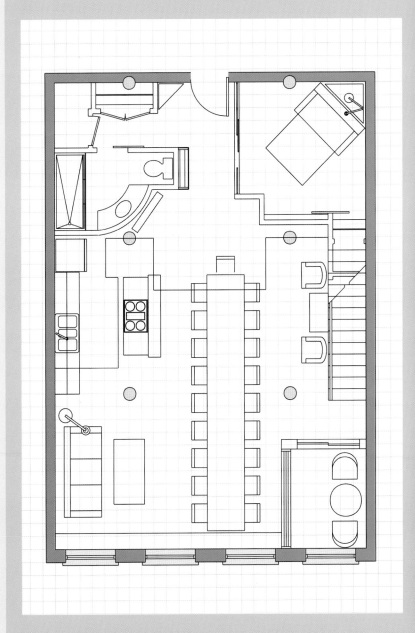

Chapter Six

The Mechanics of Your Loft

With the floor plan complete, you can turn your drawings over to a contractor and feel fairly confident that the finished product will be what you designed. If you want to delve a little deeper into the actual construction process, read this section to understand the lifeblood operations in your loft—things we take for granted and don't often think about, but which when properly addressed, can increase our enjoyment of a space tenfold.

Rarely seen in gentrified surroundings, mechanical, electrical, plumbing, and soundproofing systems can consume the biggest chunk of your budget. While all these topics would appear to fall under the heading "mechanical," that term is reserved in this book for heating and cooling systems.

‹ *Restored to a condition recalling its construction, the concertina-barred radiators under the windows and a central ceiling fan comprise the mechanical, or heating and cooling system, in this archetypal loft.*

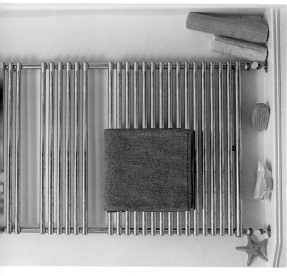

Heating

When we think of heating, the first thing that comes to mind is a **furnace,** but you have other choices available that may be more appropriate to use with hard-surfaced floors. **Radiant heat** works like the sun—heat is absorbed by walls or floors, and then radiated when needed back into the room.

◆ **"In-floor" heating systems,** as the name implies, are coils buried in or under the floor that project uniform heat.

◆ **Traditional furnaces** are no longer huge dinosaurs looming in the basement—or usurping valuable square footage in your loft. Units are now available that can take up air space by sitting on top of a capped bathroom enclosure, discreetly masked with a drywall enclosure or alternate screening. Or they can be removed from your loft and installed on the roof or other remote location. They're compact, quiet, and remarkably efficient.

◆ If your loft is set up for **hot water heat** with ancient radiators, be happy. It's one of the cleanest, most inexpensive, and reliable sources of heat. With the addition of **bi-directional ceiling fans** to push hot air back down, you can achieve seasonal comfort in keeping with the era of warehouse buildings. Beautifully embossed with ornate details or sculptural in style, they come in every dimension imaginable, from huge behemoths previously used in hospitals or schools to tiny, elegant wall-hung models. If their "found" condition is too rustic for your taste, an auto body shop will sandblast off the old paint and reapply a car-quality color of your choice for a nominal fee.

> *Regardless of the cooling system you select, fans are always beneficial. Sitting under a ceiling fan on a hot day can make a 10-degree difference in room temperature. It will keep cooled air circulating, so you can set your air conditioner's thermostat to as much as 8 degrees lower with the same level of cooling comfort, providing an average six percent savings on air conditioning costs.*

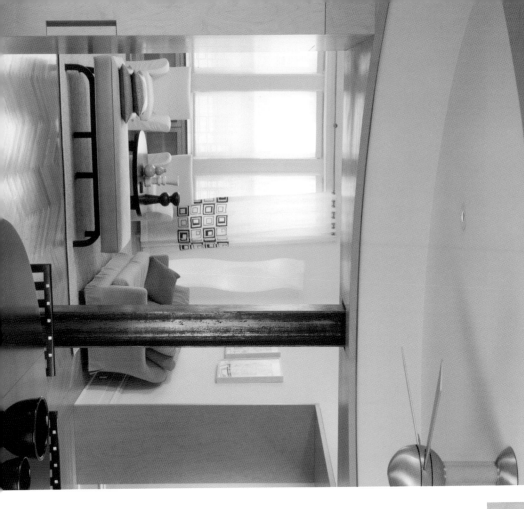

< The continuous production of radiators in Europe has led to innovations in design to keep up with the demands of the new loft market. Coils, grids, and hoops have elevated a heat source to an art form.

> A grand entrance rotunda moonlights as a sophisticated dining room. With concealed hinges and touch-latch door openers, wood veneered walls flanking the room at one end conceal storage while maintaining the clean lines.

Cooling

Heating and air conditioning are opposing functions and should be given individual attention regardless of which heat delivery system you select. Forcing air through the same ducts will limit the effectiveness of one or both systems. Warm air rises and cool air falls. Therefore, heating should emanate from floor level, whereas the cooling should be concentrated at the ceiling. Don't let the builder talk you into the heating and air conditioning being delivered to you in the same ceiling ducts—your feet will freeze in winter, and you'll be a hothead in summer! A dedicated blower used only for air conditioning will be more effective, and with ducts exposed for that industrial look, the installation costs are reduced.

Windows

Unquestionably the most sought after element of lofts, windows can also be the Achilles' heel. Try a couple of simple improvements before embarking on a replacement quest. In the end, what we all aspire to is the look of the **authentic** windows with the **efficiency** of replacements.

◆ **If the windows don't have to be opened** or serve as emergency exits, lock and caulk them closed. When dealing with double panes, ensure that the inside window is sealed more tightly than the outside one or you'll encounter condensation as the warm air becomes trapped between the panes. Weatherproof the inner sash to prevent air leakage—a bevy of tiny gaps is the equivalent of an open window. Some recommend adding an interior storm window or a sheet of Plexiglas, creating an air gap between layers for insulation, but I find condensation can become a more annoying problem, making it a less than satisfactory solution. You're better off with dramatic draperies backed with insulated lining.

◆ **Your exposure to the sun** and the interior finishes play a big part in attaining comfortable interior temperatures. North-facing properties or those blocked from the sun by other tall buildings can experience a more significant temperature difference than their neighbors on the south side. Concrete, ceramic, and stone floors all absorb heat from the sun and radiate it back into the room long after the sun has set, yet they are inherently cold surfaces. Wood is a more constant material, unless exposed to extremes.

< New windows with a "Low-E" coating are like sunscreens for your home. If you calculate what you could save on heating, cooling, curtains, and replacement furnishings due to color fading and wear, the window expenditure would no doubt pay for itself in a short period of time.

< In retrofits, the existing windows are often severely damaged, but as the defining feature of an industrial building they're worth a valiant effort with caulk or new insulated glass before shopping for replacements.

◆ **When replacements are a foregone conclusion,** plan on windows that appeal to you and suit the building, then try matching them up with products on the market, or price them out as custom units. The choices available are daunting and the accompanying costs exorbitant, but when you're dealing with a large quantity, the cost of specialty units to replicate the existing ones may be the same as standard windows.

◆ **Unless you live in a tropical climate,** a minimum of two layers of glazing is necessary. Better yet are triple glazed windows with a "Low-E" ("low emission") coating. A metallic oxide coating on the interior glass panel cuts down on the transfer of heat and ultraviolet rays from the sun. They are usually combined with argon gas between the panels, which increases energy efficiency and muffles sound without affecting your perception of the outside vista.

A particular loft in Chicago comes to mind: it sits right next to an eight-lane highway. Over a pleasant cup of coffee in idyllic surroundings, I asked a resident if he used the balcony much, to which he

replied, "See for yourself." When I stepped out the door the noise was so deafening, I retreated immediately. The windows were made of triple-pane glass. Between each sheet of glazing is an air space that insulates the loft from sound and exterior temperatures.

◆ **All windows are labeled with "U-values"** rating the amount of ultraviolet light infiltration (the lower the better) and "R-values" for their insulating capacity (the higher the better). Glass is a highly heat conductive material and operable windows have many paths where air leakage can occur. Frames should be constructed of a nonconducting material such as wood, regardless of the protective coating applied to the finished surface. Commercial windows will blend into the exterior of industrial buildings and are available with the same features of residential styles.

Sample Average "R" Values

TYPE	VALUE	NOTES
Single-Pane Glass	0.96	
Double-Pane Glass	2.04	
Triple-Pane Glass	3.23	
Brick Walls	0.82	with 4" (102 mm) fiberglass batts 15.00
Concrete Block Walls	2.05	with insulation 6.12

The objective of any HVAC system is to provide an environment that is held constant at a comfortable level, normally 72° F (22° C). Air flows from a hotter area to a colder one and insulation is designed to reduce that passage. In warm climates, when it's 90° F (32° C) outside and 70° F (21° C) inside, heat will flow into your space at every opportunity, thereby causing heat gain. Conversely, when it's freezing outside, heat will escape from the inside, causing heat loss. **Walls and windows allow a certain amount of heat transfer, which is measured and referred to as the R-value** (or RSI-value). Every building material you purchase will have an R-value. The higher the value, the slower the rate of heat transfer through the insulating material.

Insulation

Insulating an exterior wall can trim heating and cooling costs by as much as 20 to 40 percent, which is why many fabulous old brick walls end up covered with sheetrock.

Before racing ahead to insulate and cover the old brick walls, find out how they were made. Some of these walls were constructed using an exterior wall of brick, an air space, then an interior wall of brick. The triple-layer construction may provide sufficient protection from the infiltration of unwanted air. Or you can look into a blown-in insulation that would fill the void—just instruct the installer to use a gentle pressure, too much can dislodge the interior wall, particularly if it's in a fragile condition.

My first loft conversion was of an old mill into our design studio. The building sat on a canal, unprotected on all sides with outstanding single glazed, multi-paned, 14-foot (4.3 meter) high windows. The building also had single brick walls layered with the accumulation of more than 100 years of paint. Sandblasting seemed like the most expedient way to remove it. Well, let me tell you, I've never felt dirtier or more exhausted. So it was understandable that once the paint was gone, we moved in. What I didn't realize was that when you sandblast brick you weaken the composition and remove the factory fired protective layer, like having your face abraded. And that no matter how many times you vacuum the walls, you'll never be rid of residual sand. Every time there was a strong wind it was like being in a sandstorm on the Sahara Desert: a thin coat of fine-grained sand covered everything and the wind whistled through the weakened mortar.

If you sandblast, apply a sealer to the wall after. It will darken the brick slightly whether you use paste wax, shellac, or silicone, and the surface will have a slight sheen.

> Yes folks, that would be me filling bags with sand after it has been blasted at the walls. I will never do that again, but the walls do look great!

> My resolve failed when we got to the ceiling: balancing on a scaffold with a pressure hose firing sand over 2,000 square feet (185.5 square meters) was beyond me. I hired a painter to spray the ceiling.

> Covering the walls and adding insulation was anathema to me: I'd rather freeze. And sometimes I thought we would.

> My vision encompassed low drywall partition walls, sleek furnishings, and state-of-the-art halogen lighting contrasted against worn wood floors, towering wood columns, and exposed brick walls. My vision was realized; I was just too tired to photograph it for posterity.

^ Simple, modern solutions compose a practical bathroom. Rolling files for individual guest use are designed to accommodate cosmetic travel bags. Cutouts in the stone vanity face serve as towel repositories. Built into the mirror assembly are task lights to augment the natural light from transoms. Insulation installed in the walls reduces noise significantly; your loft will remain a sanctuary even with guests.

Ventilation

Vent fans to evacuate moisture are imperative, even when you have new replacement windows. Moisture is generated inside your loft by your very presence, through the act of breathing, as well as from cooking, washing, plants, and big offenders such as whirlpool tubs and showers. In old structures, moisture infiltrates from the exterior. After a rainstorm, brick, block, or stone walls absorb water, and when exposed to the hot sun, vapor pressure drives moisture to the cooler interior.

In new construction, **air exchangers** are installed by code to ensure an even and constant replacement of air, but they don't negate the need for exhaust of extraneous moisture build-up from kitchens and baths. There are several factors you need to consider for the efficient expulsion of moisture. Look for fans that exhaust to the outside via a wall vent, or through a central duct to the roof. Determine the proper size motor you need to calculate the CFM, which stands for cubic feet per minute of air transfer by using the chart below. Most state and government regulations follow specific minimum recommendations (see chart, page 131).

Minimum CFM Recommendations
Kitchen: 15 Air Changes Per Hour
Bathroom: 8 Air Changes Per Hour
Laundry: 6 Air Changes Per Hour

Take into consideration the path of the air to the outside. Long runs, multiple bends and turns, and the type of duct will all affect the ease of air flow, or static pressure. **Fans** are rated at 0 static pressure. For each 10 feet (3 meters) of rigid duct, elbow, wall, or roof cap, add .10 static pressure, for 4" (107 mm) duct add .04, and add .06 for 6" (152 mm) ridged duct. Flexible duct, if not stretched out completely, creates much greater static and therefore decreases CFM. For example, if you are venting at the roof and making one turn along the way the calculation is as follows:

20 feet (6.1 meters) of 6" (152 mm) duct	= .12 inch static
1 elbow	= .10
1 grille	= .10
1 roof cap	= .10
Total	= .42 inch

Combining the two exercises, we know that we require a fan at least 106.6 CFM at .42 static. Always round up in matching figures to fan motors and keep in mind that wider ducts reduce the noise, so if you have the choice, go with a six-inch (152 mm) installation over a four (107 mm). We're all too familiar with bathroom fans that seemingly do nothing but make a lot of noise. Sound is measured in sones, the lower the figure the quieter the model. Sones drop dramatically the further away from the face grill that the motor is mounted. Look for a supplier who actually has the model installed so you can perform a simple test. Hold a tissue up to the grill to see how much suction is being generated, and obviously you'll be able to hear how loud it is.

Calculating the CFM

Take the cubic feet of the room multiplied by the number of air changes divided by 60 minutes per hour. For example:

◆ A bath 10 feet wide by 10 feet long by 8 feet high (3 meters by 3 meters by 2.4 meters) equals 800 cubic feet (23 cubic meters)

◆ 800 multiplied by 8 (air changes) equals 6,400

◆ 6,400 divided by 60 (minutes per hour) equals 106.6 minimum CFM fan required; for each additional 2 feet (.6 meters) of ceiling height add 25 percent to the required CFM

< Even in elaborate, open concept lofts, the problem of moisture accumulation needs to be addressed to avoid mold, mildew, condensation on windows, or just a general feeling of cold because moisture absorbs heat from the area as well as your body. Ceiling exhaust fans located between the shower and whirlpool bath will extract moisture from the air before it infiltrates the rest of the loft.

> Systems are available that can exhaust several rooms at once and all you see is an unobtrusive circular grille several inches in diameter on the wall or ceiling. They come equipped with dampers (a small flip door) that closes when the fan is not in operation, preventing infiltration of air from the outside.

Kitchen Exhaust

Kitchen **hood fans** operate under the same principles and data for each model will include CFMs, which rate their exhaust capacity and "sones" for noise level, and an efficiency rating. The primary consideration is the amount of air required to evacuate smoke, odors, heat, and moisture. This will vary with the type of cooking appliance, your mode of cooking, and the style of the hood fan.

For routine preparation with the stove **positioned** against an exterior wall, a wall mount hood will suffice. For open cooktops on an island or peninsula, multiple appliances under one hood, or heavy cooking, your CFM requirements will increase exponentially to the point where you may need additional ventilator control housings, better known as filters, to handle the load. This doesn't mean installing two hood fans beside each other. You can purchase the appropriate motor, or blower, as they're referred to, and have the surrounding hood manufactured to your design at around the same cost of a prefabricated unit.

< Serious chefs require updraft ventilation that provides the best overall performance, capturing smoke and heat as they rise. Look for units that have layered mesh filters that remove easily for cleaning and can fit in a dishwasher, and make sure it's equipped with built-in lighting.

> A restaurant exhaust fan suits the eclectic style of this loft kitchen. The clinical appearance of stainless steel is offset with a whimsical piecrust counter edge and a ceramic backsplash festooned with softly colored thumbprints.

Hood fans are designed as extractors or recirculators. Extractors draw kitchen vapors and grease through an activated charcoal filter and then out into the open air or into a ventilation shaft, which is the most efficient method, while recirculators return the air into the room after it has passed through the filter. To keep any hood fan operating at maximum capacity, the filter should be cleaned regularly and replaced once a year, a detail easily overlooked—you know the saying—time flies when you're having fun!

5 Tips for Choosing a Hood Fan

1 The hood should be as large as possible to reduce smoke from high heat, air turbulence, and drafts.

2 Optimally, the width of the hood will overlap the cooking surface by 6 inches (152 mm) and, at the very least, cover the cooktop.

3 Indoor barbecues must be vented to the outdoors and be completely covered by the hood, with the intake centered over the unit.

4 Mounting heights measured from the countertop to the top of the hood can vary from 28 inches (711 mm) for an under-cabinet model to 62 inches (1,575 mm) for an island installation over a barbecue.

5 Downdraft ventilators are built into the countertop with the blower installed in the cabinet below, or in a remote location such as a closet in an adjoining room.

Sound

Our attraction to loft living in busy downtown cores comes at a price—the barrage of constant noise. Taken from the Latin word "nausea" and defined as unwanted sound, noise is a direct assault on our senses and can seriously affect the enjoyment of our dream loft. Honking horns, squealing brakes, and construction jackhammers are all part of city life. Coupled with the absence of walls that absorb and contain sound, noise becomes a critical issue to be dealt with. The biggest offenders are single pane windows—replace them with triple pane thermal glazing to eliminate street din.

When starting from scratch, it's easy to take precautions during the construction period. The benefits you'll reap far outweigh the effort involved—most people just don't realize how easy it is to mount a defense against noise, both on the interior and exterior.

When all else fails, turn sound to your advantage by masking the unwanted noise with a version that pleases your ears. It could be music piped in from a single source to multiple speakers appropriately spaced throughout the loft and controlled with a remote. An aquarium emits that comforting gurgle, as does a sound machine. I have one that friends gave me to travel with that replicates a waterfall, a rainstorm, a babbling brook, and ocean waves crashing on the beach. It works every time to drown out the late night sirens that are part and parcel of urban life.

∧ Water in motion is the quintessential relaxant, transcending the physical limitations of the loft. Constructed the same way as a shower from a plywood form, waterproof gasket, and poured concrete, not only will extraneous noise disappear, but a feeling of calm will prevail.

9 Tips for Soundproofing

1. Use resilient caulk at corner, ceiling, and floor joints.

2. On partition walls, stagger the studs so they don't face each other and fill the gap with glass fiber insulation to cut sound transmission.

3. Offset light switches and receptacles in lieu of mounting them back-to-back to nullify vibration.

4. Builders often leave larger openings than necessary to enable pre-manufactured windows to be easily installed. The resulting gap is concealed behind the window trim. By removing the casing, filling the space with insulation, and caulking the edges, you'll have closed off another point of entry for street noise.

5. The same principles apply to finished ceilings. Who wants to hear their neighbor above go through his morning ablutions, or your guest in the bathroom below your lofted bedroom? Sound can travel through the smallest of openings, from floor-to-floor, through ceiling light fixtures, holes made for plumbing pipes, electrical wires, and ducts.

6. Install insulated doors equipped with rubber gaskets around their perimeter to seal noise from corridors, laundry rooms, and washrooms.

7. Closets and bathrooms provide a sound buffer when positioned against a corridor or bedroom wall.

8. Flexible insulation sprayed around pipes will eliminate vibration and the transfer of sound to wallboard, or wrap them with batting. Use flexible duct with blowers located away from the point of entry.

9. Soft furnishings, heavy draperies, carpeting or area rugs, even plants will absorb the high-frequency noise levels. If ceiling noise is a problem, suspend baffles covered in your choice of fabric to cut the noise made from insulation panels. Drop an insulated sheetrock ceiling over your conversation area to reduce reverberation. Drape heavy fabrics across the ceiling in a matching color to disappear or a contrast shade for a design statement.

> Adding another layer of sheetrock to existing walls and leaving a gap between the two considerably reduces sound transmission. Applied with careful finesse, rectilinear cement board normally reserved for wet installations imparts a distinctive identity. The visual and tactile are simultaneously addressed with the installation of recessed lights between the wallboard panels.

Lighting

Lighting is a passion of mine, so you'll have to pardon me for one moment while I wax poetically on the subject. Nothing can transform the most mundane space into an ethereal sanctuary or the commonest person into a vision of glamour than lighting. Functioning below the level of consciousness, it affects not only how we look and perceive our surroundings, but how we feel. A good exercise is to visit your favorite restaurant and then stop at a donut shop. I guarantee that the latter will be brilliantly lit with harsh fluorescents, an excellent ploy to keep patrons from lingering on the premises and to protect employees from late night predators. By contrast, the dining room will stroke you with its seductive ambience, enticing you to linger over courses and relish fine wines. Lighting is hypnotic and what amazes me about it is that regardless of the decor or the music, we all look and feel better.

Basic lighting design can be broken down into three main areas: **ambient lighting,** which is general, diffused illumination; **task lighting,** which is concentrated light for working; and **accent lighting,** which highlights details.

Understanding the psychological impact that light has on perception of our environment, manufacturers have developed bulbs that "read" color differently. We tend to think of objects as having a fixed color, when in reality the appearance results from the way it reflects and absorbs the light that is falling on it. Hence the experience of purchasing an item under the controlled lighting of a store and discovering it looks completely different when we get it home.

The source and placement of light within your loft will have a direct influence on what the final space looks and feels like. This is a complicated business, but with some basic choices and general information I can hopefully guide you through to a satisfactory resolution.

^ Non-uniform lighting projects a feeling of intimacy and develops a character as it draws you into the loft. Serenity segues into high drama with accent lighting on significant details. The space appears clean and uncluttered.

Ambient Lighting

Most familiar is ambient lighting, commonly associated with the ceiling fixture that washes over an area with general, diffused illumination and can be accomplished with simple, elemental lamps. Incandescent lamps are the original electric light invented more than one hundred years ago. A tungsten wire filament is encased inside a glass bulb, an electric current is passed through the filament, and resistance causes it to "incandesce" or glow. The common light bulb or "A" lamp falls into this category as do "R" lamps, so designated because of their reflective abilities; "Par" lamps coined from the parabolic shape of the bulb, they look like an auto headlight; and fluorescent lamps.

While R and Par lamps have the advantage of beam control, the common link between incandescent lamps is their color rendition that is in the diluted warm spectrum even with so-called "cool" fluorescents. For uniform lighting, the fixtures are generally arranged in a symmetrical pattern, but in a residential scenario most of us just want ambient light to direct us through the space with a flick of a switch. However, this is a boring solution—better to illuminate an interior partition wall or architectural details to act as cornerstones.

Low-ceilinged areas, such as a kitchen below an upper mez-zanine, can be elevated visually with ambient lighting. Fluor-escent fixtures installed between the exposed joists of an unfinished ceiling or in a cove around the perimeter will uniformly illuminate the ceiling, giving the illusion of additional height and emitting a soft glow at night.

Task Lighting

Task lighting, as the name suggests, is working lighting, be it under-cabinet fixtures in a kitchen to highlight counter functions, lamps for reading, or bathroom mirror brilliance. The beam of light is directed at a relatively small area so that we can concentrate on the task at hand without distraction from our surroundings. "MR16" or low voltage lamps as they're known, are most efficient at accomplishing this because of their precise beam control, which eliminates shadows on the task area and prevents glare from spilling into the surrounding. Test this out yourself by reading in a dark room with fixtures equipped with an "A" lamp and an "MR16" bulb. The difference is amazing.

> Natural light is balanced or augmented with artificial ambient light, particularly important in lofts where the inner core is dim. Paper shaded floor lamps, inverted and suspended over a dining room table cleverly address the scale of this loft.

< The advantage of contrasting lighting is exemplified in bath-rooms. Ambient light emanating from the ceiling fixture washes the room in soft color, whereas halogen lamps recessed into a bulkhead skirting the room provide crisp white illumination for reading or applying makeup.

< (far left) Uniform levels of ambient light establish a feeling of bland spaciousness.

< (left) With the addition of accent lighting, dark recesses contrast against brilliant light directed at details.

✓ **Floors beyond repair** have an upside—recessed pot lights can be installed under a sub-floor or into newly poured concrete to illuminate up onto columns and walls. In a loft with moderate height ceilings, or those that have been gentrified with drywall, the floor illumination of structural columns should suffice. Enormous vaults would benefit from both illumination directed up into the ceiling void and column lighting originating from the floor or ceiling.

✓ **Wall sconces** can become an emphatic feature combining both architectural interest and illumination, supplementing or replacing overhead ambient fixtures. The fixtures that house the lamps can be directional to beam light up into the ceiling, down onto a column, or both ways if there's an opening at the top and bottom of the sconce. With a light emitting face, they can provide more general illumination. Think about what kind of light you want, either ambient or accent, and where you want the light to go to establish placement for the wall electrical box. Personal preference and the size of the actual housing come into play—just keep three things in mind: eye level is 5 feet 6 inches (1,676 mm), so if the sconce itself is a focal point, keep it in your range of vision; the illusion is spoiled if the light bulb is visible and; sconces protrude from the wall, so position deep ones higher, away from head and shoulders to avoid mishaps.

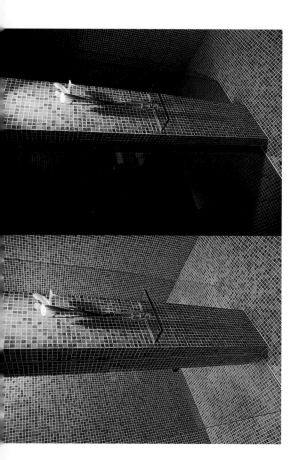

Accent Lighting

Accent lighting is the last of the lighting components that should be included in every installation, but is most often overlooked by amateurs. It provides the texture, drama, and punch to interior design by allowing details to dominate the landscape. Experience the joy of sipping a glass of wine in candlelight and gazing into the vast loft space above you. With no lighting, you won't see a thing; with the wrong lighting you'll flood the whole room—hardly conducive to intimate conversation. The Picasso on the wall will blend in with the background if it's cloaked in darkness.

To be effective, accent lighting must distinguish itself from other illumination in the room and the MR16 lamp is the singular choice. Low-voltage lamps, like the MR16, have a crisp white light in contrast to the dull, yellow hue provided by "A" lamps or fluorescents.

With your floor plan in hand, visualize what walls are going to need attention with illumination. Custom features such as a pond or waterfall will become animated at night with submerged lighting. Try to think of the space as a drama unfolding before you. Variance in the light will create a collection of ever changing shapes promulgated by the light radiation. The space will take on a deeper significance by the intriguing interaction of light and shadow.

> Track or cable lighting is the most flexible solution, because it allows you to add lights and adjust focus easily. The zany twists of a cable system add levity to a very linear kitchen. Lamps are positioned to illuminate the intricate tin ceiling and distinct steel columns that punctuate the cabinetry.

At this point in the planning process the fixtures themselves aren't important, just the fact of their existence is what matters, so you can add their location to your plan ensuring the electrician puts electrical boxes, switches, and receptacles where you need them.

An **electrical plan** is a copy of your floor plan, leaving only permanent elements that intersect the floor, such as walls and columns. Line this up with the plan you've created thus far so that you can see the furnishings underneath. Using a computer is much easier for this, as you can tile one plan over another. Determine and mark on this new plan where you want lamps for reading, and other task lighting as well as any wall sconces or recessed floor fixtures.

Create a **"reflected ceiling"** plan by copying the floor plan again and adding any details that impact the ceiling, such as columns, ductwork, or full-height walls. As the name implies, this plan is like looking at the ceiling through a mirror. Again, layer this over the furniture plan to determine where ambient, task, or accent lights will originate from the ceiling. This will include track fixtures and dining room chandeliers as well as ceiling fans. With the right combination of light, the dullest of enclosures will float in its landscape, perpetrating a sense of spatial mystery.

> *Locate any specialty receptacles on the electrical plan, especially when furniture is positioned off the walls, calling for a floor receptacle. An extension cord snaking across the floor would seriously undermine this precise suite.*

< *Critically assess what is suitable for dramatic emphasis—by highlighting everything you defeat the purpose. Located at the end of a corridor, the illumination of a wall niche draws our attention.*

Discreet and graceful **picture lights** equipped with halogen lamps that attach to the wall or a picture frame and operate with a plug, calling for a recessed receptacle, referred to as a "clock" receptacle are now available. Eye level for hanging art is also considered 5 feet 6 inches (1,676 mm) at the center so position the outlet accordingly to allow for flexibility in what you hang.

Planning the Placement of Lights

Placement of lights is determined in the planning stage, so they can be "hard wired" directly into an electrical box recessed into the wall or ceiling and operated with a switch. Don't dismay if you're dealing with finished space. A single existing ceiling box can electrify 12 feet (3.7 meters) of track lighting, or a series of recessed ceiling pots. While more time consuming and consequently costly, a qualified electrician can "fish" wires from behind the sheetrock skin or floor to wire and switch fixtures. The appeal of a wall sconce is somewhat diminished when a cord is exposed. You can also build freestanding units, such as a slim drywall box in front of a wall to house recessed up-lights, achieving the same results as wall wash fixtures installed in a ceiling.

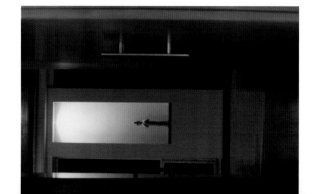

Integrated Audio/Visual Elements

Thoughts about a design program are usually dominated by domestic considerations—furniture, kitchen and bathroom layouts, color, fabric, and style. Designers think on a broader scale to include enhancements that will elevate the experience of living as close to an ideal of perfection as possible.

Think about what we do when we're totally harried, planning a romantic evening, entertaining guests, having a dinner party—we turn down the lights and turn up the music. Integrated sound is a system that emanates audio, and in some cases video functions, from one source to speakers throughout the loft, and is operated via a remote control and a small pad on the wall, which is equipped with an electronic eye to pick up the signal.

To consider this as a grandiose scheme achievable only by wealthy patrons would be to cheat yourself. You can wire in the construction stage, at an average cost of about $500 for a 6,000 square foot (557 square meter) area, then install the components as funds become available. Audiophiles who've sworn off the convenience of multi-room audio because it compromises sound quality should revisit the idea. Constantly improving technology due to consumer demand now preserves the quality of the sound signal over long distances, delivering clarity to our ears. I hate to admit it, but live performances have lost some of their thrill—the sound is never comparable to my home system. Forget elevator "musak."

^ A discreet white keypad positioned over the desk (back right of image) can activate multiple audio functions at the source or from across the loft with a remote control.

› *Mechanics that are disguised as art, such as the exceptional Bang & Olufsen products that are amongst the elite displayed in the permanent collection of The Museum of Modern Art in New York, are worthy of a place of prominence in the loft. Functional boxes can be housed remotely in a closet, freeing up prestigious space.*

Evaluate Your Audio/Visual Needs

The first priority is to evaluate where you would appreciate listening to music or news. In my situation, I would chose the kitchen, living/dining area, master bathroom, bedroom, and office area. Follow-up with a trip to several equipment suppliers to see what's available on the market, what type of system you'd choose if money were no object, and what the wiring requirements are. Reputable companies who've been around a long time can be counted on to maintain compatibility of components over the years, but don't feel compelled to select only one manufacturer. I've put together integrated systems for large installations that have utilized a variety of products, representative of the best in each category for a particular location. Look at the ease of operation with integrated units. Can a single remote operate a full product palette? As a technologically challenged individual, I insist on ease of operation, having

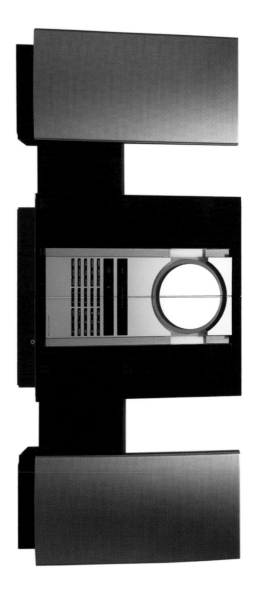

been exposed to too many installations where manuals, multiple remotes, and a degree in rocket science were required to play a CD. Owners became servants to the technology instead of vice versa. Mull over how visible speakers will impact your furniture layout, and where the most convenient placement would be for the receiver. Many manufacturers are now designing their equipment to resemble art, such as the exceptional Bang & Olufsen products, which can be displayed as part of the design, rather than be hidden in a closet.

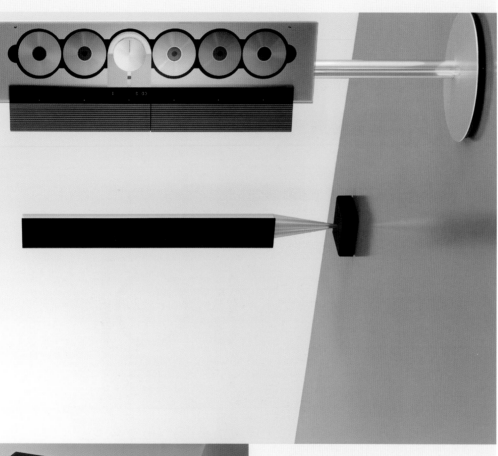

^ Should you be unfortunate enough to own a mammoth television, I want you to go into a corner and give yourself a spanking! My life has been spent trying to integrate these monsters into otherwise gracious environments. Be a true urbanite and head to the cinema when you need life-size video.

Rapid developments in software have dramatically changed the face of "High-Fi" equipment. Just when audio/video equipment threatened to take over our residences by their size alone, pioneers presented compact, multifunctional alternatives.

Plan Your System Layout

Take into consideration the size and layout of your loft, the ceiling height, and the construction when deliberating over speakers and placement. Small, open lofts may only require one set of speakers properly positioned to flood the area with sound. The same loft with closed off bedroom quarters would use two sets. In a shared building, your neighbors will appreciate you more with sound levels geared to a single area instead of blaring speakers trying to reach every corner of your loft! High, wooden ceilings and beams indicative of the flooring below will resonate like a guitar, making clarity of sound take precedence over output. The acoustics in a partitioned loft encased in insulated drywall will require more speakers. In addition, outdoor speakers on your terrace will help diffuse street noise.

Read up on the latest and greatest on the market and make a wish list of how your ideal system would function, then take your floor plan, complete with room heights, to an established dealer to help in the selection and location of components. There is so much on the market these days. Don't get discouraged if someone tells you there's no such thing as what you want—try the next guy.

Having established the receiver and speaker locations, you need to locate the wall pads that are the key to operating each set of speakers. The keypad can be manipulated manually with your fingertips or with a remote handset to select simple functions such as the equipment you want to operate, where it's operational, and volume control, to sophisticated tasks such as security, climate control, or lighting levels. As a reward for your perseverance, install a control at your bed so you can switch off every sound in the loft. Following the electrical lines to the light switches makes the most sense, allowing the cables to be bundled together and the mechanical plates grouped in one location. Critical to the smooth functioning of the system is the isolation of the keypads by a solid barrier, be it a partition wall or a column. Infrared rays from remote controls are so adept at picking up commands over a broad spectrum of space that functions instigated at one location will be acted on by every other keypad within visible distance. Equipped with the appropriate wire and staples, you can link the system in an afternoon.

Photograph your accomplishment, then measure and draw a diagram of the wire locations. Thus armed, you can wallboard with confidence knowing that as funds become available you can start adding the components to fulfill your sound mission. An integrated system of quality components will not only distribute sound throughout your loft, it will elevate it to the custom league substantially adding to the resale value.

Electrical Symbols

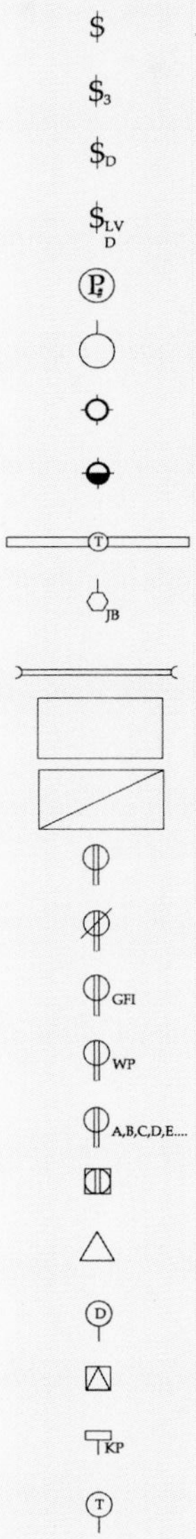

Switch
3-Way Switch
Dimmer Switch
Low Voltage Dimmer Switch
Surface Mounted Incandescent Light Fixture
Wall Mounted Incandescent Light Fixture
Recessed Light Fixture
Recessed Directional Light Fixture
Track Light Fixture
Junction Box for Cable Light
Fluorescent Strip Light
Surface Mounted Fluorescent Light
Recessed Fluorescent Light
Duplex Receptacle
Duplex Receptacle at Nonstandard Height
Duplex Receptacle with Ground Fault Interrupter
Waterproof Duplex Receptacle
Specialty Receptacle
Floor Mounted Duplex Receptacle
Telephone Receptacle
Data Receptacle
Floor Mounted Telephone Receptacle
Control Key Pad
Thermostat

A basic electrical plan will designate the location of the stereo receiver for radio transmission, televisions, phones, fax, and Internet for cable service.

The Finishing Touches

Combine your electrical plans with your floor plans and you are ready to start the physical work.

Reflected Ceiling Plan: Mezzanine Level

The plan indicates where lights, fans, ventilation units—anything electrical—are located. Think about the disparate moods you've created with lighting and how they will interface when connecting them to switches. If you want lighting that is focused on partition walls to come on all at once to guide your passage, put them on one switch. Utilize dimmer switches for ultimate control.

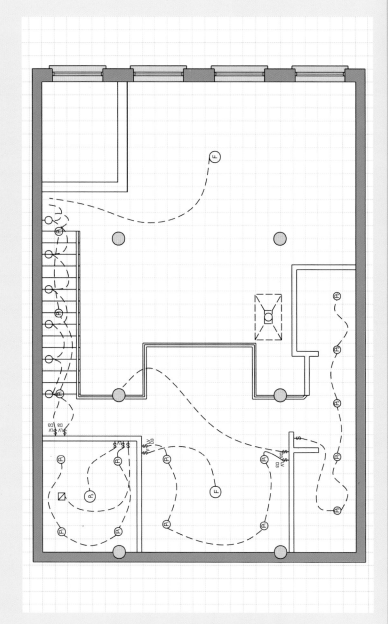

Electrical Plan: Mezzanine Level

The same plan is copied again. The electrical plan indicates where you would like particular receptacles, cable for television, the Internet, phones—anything that is powered in the walls or floor. The electrician will add general receptacles in random locations to augment your specialty ones.

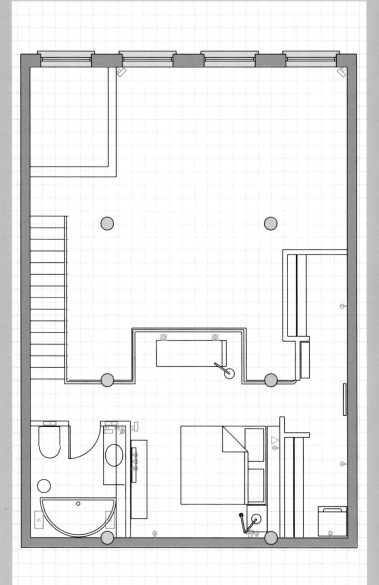

Reflected Ceiling Plan: Main Level

Inexpensive during construction, two-way switches—called double pole—provide you the convenience of operating lights in two locations. For example, stairway illumination can be switched on and off at the bottom and top of the stairs. Group multiple switches together for a clean look.

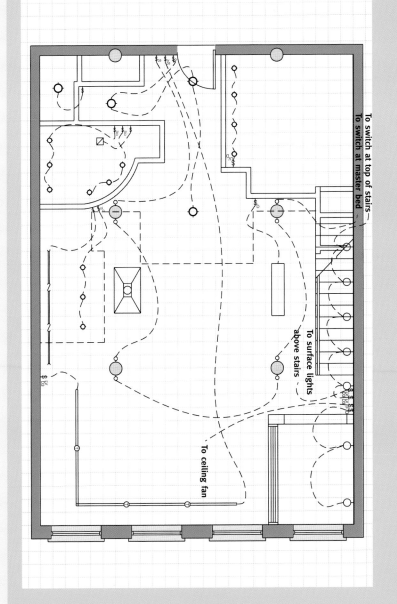

To switch at top of stairs
To switch at master bed

To surface lights above stairs

To ceiling fan

Electric Plan: Main Level

The kitchen demands the most specific electrical requirements. Don't forget to request power on islands—a receptacle on the side, behind a flip-down drawer front, or a pop-up version that is recessed into the island top. If you've selected your appliances, include the model numbers and pertinent volts and watts for the electrician to refer to.

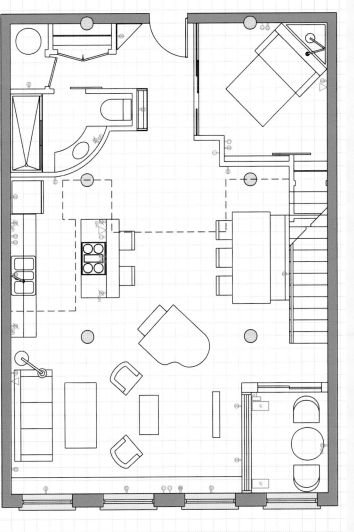

Chapter Seven

Living the Dream

Ahhh, and now for the really difficult part of the design process...how much is your dream going to cost? I hate to say it, but probably more than you think. In loft developments that are under construction, be they new or old buildings, your first stop with plans in hand will be the developer of the project.

With his workers already on site and fully expecting to count your loft among the ones they're going to finish, it's a logical starting point. The builder/developer has a vested interest in seeing that the work is done in a timely fashion and to a certain standard that will reflect positively on the entire project; and your loft could be an excellent marketing device to show potential buyers. This works well in areas with a high vacancy rate, but unfortunately, if sales are booming, you will either be left to your own devices or hit with a barrage of extra costs that far exceed the actual value of the work. Choosing to live in the center of a thriving metropolis does come with a price.

< In the loft version of hearth and home, cold hard steel is tempered with butter-colored floors and paint, a rustic brick wall, and a welcoming fire.

∧ Multifunctional built-in furnishings maximize the potential of your available space, but they require skilled craftsmen to transform the concept into a reality.

General Contractors

A general contractor is a person who will evaluate your plans, determine what workers are required to instigate the plan, and provide you with a quotation to complete the job. They handle the scheduling, the accounting, and the general review of the work. They also act as the intermediary between you and the people physically doing the construction, and are ultimately responsible for the final outcome, including warranties. Go about the process of finding a contractor in the same way we discussed selecting an architect or designer. Ask your friends. Ask your neighbors in the building.

How to Find One

Most builders and contractors belong to construction associations and you can call to get an idea of who does what in your area. You can also contact your local government-housing agency. They should have a listing of general contractors and may be able to inform you of any delinquent companies that have failed to meet minimum building standards. But I've found both these avenues can be sketchy. Construction associations are in business to promote the business of their members so the information can be biased, or simply not forthcoming. Government agencies are similarly watching their backs in our litigious society. A builder can have a million complaints made on a regular basis but it isn't until they are actually found negligent in a court of law that we are privy to their practices. Word-of-mouth is the best bet.

Decide What You Really Need

Think about how much you want to be involved in the construction process. For busy people with no time to spare, or novices to the building world, a good general contractor will handle everything. Their name is an excellent descriptor—they know all aspects of building, at least in relation to what they take on—and they hire the individual companies to exact each function. Plumbers, electricians, framers—the people who actually do the construction—are called trades or subcontractors. Large contracting firms will have the trades on staff. The general contractor will do the legwork of obtaining prices from each building discipline required to complete your plan. An itemized cost estimate will be presented to you, and I do mean estimate. Construction is based on so many variables, often out of the hands of the workers. Elements that are unknown until the work is actually begun can escalate your overall cost by 10 to 20 percent, so leave yourself a cushion. Then there are additions requested by you as the work progresses.

Is It Worth the Cost?

Every extra you add to a contract is more than likely being done at twice its actual cost. Why do we put up with this you ask? For two reasons. One, the general contractor is already working in your space and has a signed contract for a certain amount of work for a finite amount of money. So, I hate to say it, but he can charge you what he wants for any additions to that contract. This isn't always done arbitrarily. The additional funds accrued from extras can help offset things they underestimated as well as the pain and suffering imparted by additional clients. They have commitments to other owners and every increase to their prescribed workload jeopardizes their ability to keep that commitment.

The second reason we put up with the exorbitant cost of extras is panic. We can get so caught up in minutiae and the overwhelming desire to make it the best loft ever (especially when you are so close) that you throw caution to the wind. And, there will be details that present themselves over the course of construction that may well be worth the extra. If you did your planning well, try to trust your judgment. Remember, you were thinking with a clear head when you put your dream on paper. I have found that second-guessing ourselves once construction has begun is always counterproductive. It creates the snowball effect. One minor change inadvertently impacts something else, causing further alterations, and so on, and so on.

General contractors usually make their money by charging a percentage on the work being done, anywhere from 10 to 20 percent on average. A holdback of 10 percent should be deducted from every invoice you pay and put into a trust account to protect you against a lien on the property. This is a common practice and in many jurisdictions a requirement. It's a complicated issue; should a general contractor run into financial difficulty and neglect to pay the sub-trades, the 10 percent will satisfy any claims they legally make against you as owner of the loft. Check out the law in your area.

Once the price is approved, a contract should be signed that outlines the scope of the work and the projected time frame for construction. The general contractor, who will often have several projects underway at any given time, will set about scheduling in the various trades.

< At the onset when costs seem overwhelming, invest in the infrastructure of your loft first. Accoutrements such as furnishings and accessories can be added as funds allow.

^ A few signature pieces to complement a job well done is of more value than a room full of furnishings in the midst of shoddy construction.

Wearing Multiple Hats

For those with time on their hands, an understanding of the building process, and an excess of patience, you can act as the general contractor. The job of **hiring**, **scheduling**, **monitoring**, and **paying** the trades will fall to you.

5 Tips for Doing It Yourself

1 **Start with two quotes from each discipline** to keep the sub-contractors honest and working with a sharp pencil, ensuring you the optimum price if all things are equal. There are some highly specialized trades where the dollar value is a moot point—painters, paper hangers should you be so inclined, mill workers, and cabinetmakers to name a few. Their work is detailed and visible, a mediocre effort will be an eyesore for years to come. And did I put drywallers in that list? Also known as sheetrock and wallboard installers, these folks are skilled craftsmen. The trouble is, the really good ones make it look so easy. If you, like myself, have ever attempted to fill the joints between each sheet only to find that every time you painted the ceiling or wall the seam was visible, you know that these professionals are artists. So skip the lowest cost on certain areas, opting for the best work possible.

2 **Review standard contracts available from your local construction** *association* to familiarize yourself with the rights, obligations, and responsibilities of all parties.

3 **Make a list of the trades your project is going to require.**

4 **Check with the municipal building department for specific requirements,** such as work that must be done by union members in order to pass a building inspection, which is necessary for obtaining your occupancy permit.

5 **Then call in the sub-trades,** review your plans with them, in your loft if possible, and then wait for the quotes to come in. Typically sub-trades will present you with a total cost to do the work that includes both their time and the materials they will need. This is called a fixed cost contract. On jobs where there are a plethora of variables, many will ask to be paid by "time and materials." In this instance, you agree to pay the tradesman an hourly rate and to reimburse them for the cost of materials.

> The objective of loft planning is to take an area of ungainly proportions and transform it into open yet intimate settings. Defined by a central fireplace sheathed in luminous glass, reflected color is an integral part of this design—refreshingly relaxed in the elegantly cool atmosphere.

Typical Trades

Plumber
Handles everything to do with water

Electrician
Installs lights, switches, and receptacles

Drywaller
Installs wallboard over the partition framework and ceilings; applies plaster to the joints

Rough Carpenter
Makes temporary wood components such as access stairways

Framer
Constructs the hidden woodwork, such as framework for partitions

Millwork
Fabricates wood products off premise (baseboards, casings)

Finished Carpenter
Installation of all carpentry, which requires finished materials (trim, doors, windows, stairs, floors)

Mason
Installs stone, brick, tile, and glass block

Cabinet Maker
Constructs built-in cabinets, wall units, bars

It's Going to Cost *How Much?*

Adding up the total of all parts can be a deflating experience, like watching your dream float out the window. But take heart. This is the time for retrospection and reflection, followed by action.

Critically assess each quotation. If one appears way out of line to another for the same work, ask the highest bidder what drove his cost up. It may be that they included something you overlooked on your plan, but is necessary to the whole. This shows they are more interested in doing a good job for you than being the lowest bidder. Go back to the lowest bidder and confirm you're looking at "apples to apples." On sums that are consistently more than you thought, sit down with your tradespeople individually and ask what is driving the price up. Often they can help you find alternate methods to accomplish the same thing for less, or highlight features that are costly, leaving it up to you to assess how important that element is to you.

When you're satisfied that the prices are copasetic, take your contracts and march down to the building department of your municipality, purchase a building permit, and let the games begin. Be prepared to experience the full spectrum of emotions over the course of construction, from jubilation to despair. This is normal and to be expected. Be prepared for the endeavor to take much longer than expected. A good idea is to step away from the project every once and while, leave it alone for several days or a week and concentrate on something else. Add some levity to the situation by reading *A Year In Provence* by Peter Mayle. You'll rejoin the situation with renewed vigor and a better perspective.

< A loft designed in response to the urban situation transcends the physical limitations of the space. Glimpsed between columns and raw concrete, the spare design is offset with luxuriously modest fabrics that meld with the no-frills aesthetic.

NSF: Not Sufficient Funds

What do you do if the sum total of all the work is too rich for your bank account? Take a look at what your expectations are for the living environment. If you plan on making this your home for many years to come, put your immediate funds available into permanent elements and those that create the most upheaval during installation. These may include pouring a concrete underlayment over the existing floor to reduce sound penetration from your neighbor, construction of walls and different floor levels, and installation of staircases. You have until your patience wears out to add the frills.

At the other end of the spectrum are loft dwellers who see themselves moving up or on in a short period of time. Keep it simple. Put in only what will make your stay pleasant. The next buyer will want to add their own imprint to the loft and will undoubtedly have different ideas. In the conventional home market, the hardest sales are for very personalized residences. The beige home with the basics at a reasonable price is gone immediately.

The majority of loft dwellers are between both these scenarios—unsure how long they'll reside in a loft, but wanting to "live the loft dream." Ask yourself what epitomizes loft living to you. Chances are when you really think about it, you'll be able to pare down those plans to a version that is the essence of what you want your loft to be. When the dust settles, instead of thinking about what you could have had, you'll be reveling in what you do have.

The last step in the
design process—
adding color makes
the vision come alive.

**Main Floor,
My Finished Loft**

*The isometric drawing will hopefully
illustrate the concepts discussed in
the book. The communal area has
been kept neutral, relying on easily
changed furnishings and accessories for color punch. Under the
mezzanine, I've chosen to play up
the compressed space for dramatic
effect with dark walls and wood
finishes, adding concentrated color
in the bathroom for that element
of surprise.*

**Mezzanine,
My Finished Loft**

*The personal quarters were
conceived as a secluded enclave.
Much softer from the calculated
use of wood, carpet, and color,
the contrast to the main floor
intensifies the sense of intimacy.*

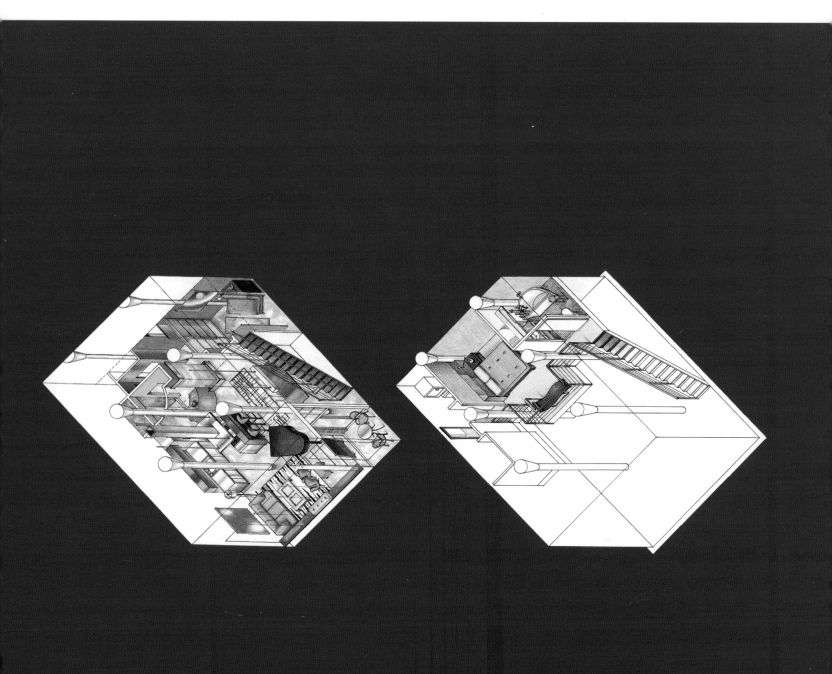

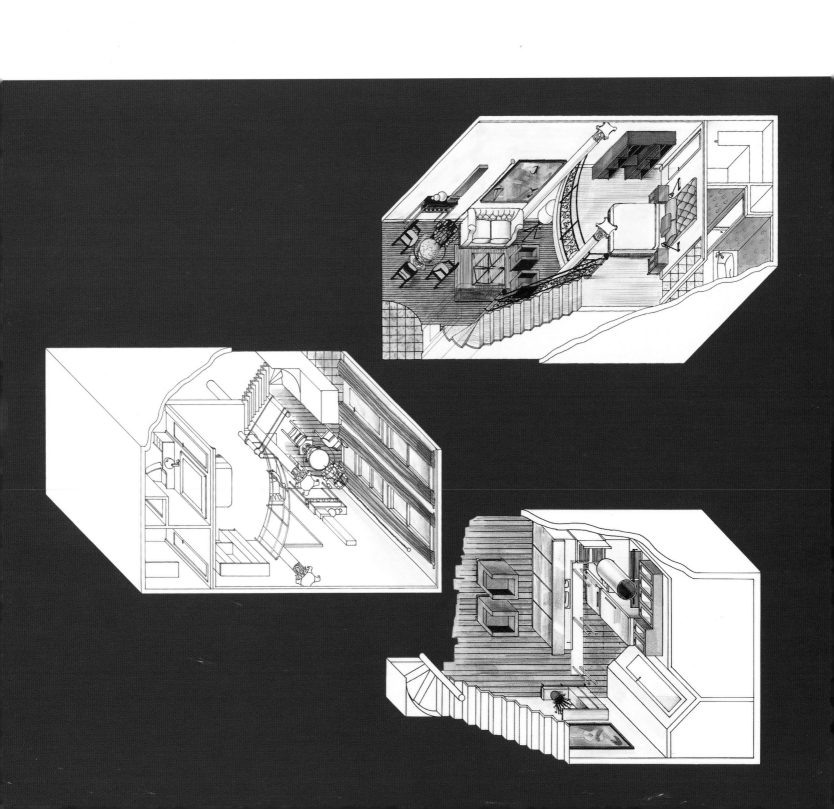

Photographer Credits

Courtesy of Agape Design, 58; 68; 70; 74

Tim Alp, 10; 11; 15; 22; 29; 31; 32 (bottom middle & right); 41; 66; 67; 75; 87; 98 (left); 100; 101 (left); 106; 138; 151

Courtesy of Artwork in Architectural Glass, 56 (top)

Courtesy of Bang & Olufsen, 143; 144

© Dan Bibb/Robert D. Henry Architects, 134; 150

Courtesy of Bisque Designer Radiators, 124

Björg, 93

Courtesy of Blanco, 52; 53; 54; 56 (middle left & right); 57 (right); 59; 60; 61; 62

Tom Bonner/Shubin + Donaldson Architects, 73; 86; 115; 126; 142; 153

Courtesy of bulthaup GmbH & Co., 24 (bottom); 45; 55; 132

Charles Callister/Fisher Freidman Associates, 8; 9; 16; 67

Morleen Doherty, 12 (left); 14

R.R. Donnelley/Studio W, 7

Courtesy of Dornbracht, 56 (bottom left); 57 (left)

© Heather Dubbeldam, Luminous Productions, 94; 95; 110; 111; 136

Esqape Design Inc., 140

Courtesy of Eventscape Inc. 85

Courtesy of Fisher & Paykel, 51

© Jeff Goldberg/Esto/Hutsachs Studio, 96; 102; 127

Eduard Hueber/Resolution 4 Architecture, 77; 97; 131 (right); 135; 139; 148

© Kretzschmer + Tomkins Photography, 104

Courtesy of The Kohler Company, 72

Nic Lehoux/Joel Berman, Design, 34

Peter Mauss/Resolution 4 Architecture, 125 (right)

Jack Miskell/Russell Project, 133

© Michael Moran Photography, Inc./Hut Sachs Studio, 64; 91

John Narvali/www.narvali.com, 90 (right); 131 (left)

Simon Paine, 30; 32 (top); 40; 63; 89; 131; 137 (right)

Courtesy of Poliform, 78; 79; 99; 109; 114; 117; 141

Cecconi Simone Interior Design Consultants, 18; 36; 48; 82; 112; 122; 154

Ernie Sparks Studios, 84; 101 (right)

Stone & Associates Ltd. Designers, 44; 107

Courtesy of Strato, SRL, 47; 116

Courtesy of Subzero, 50

Courtesy of TRE-P & TRE-Più, 99; 152

Courtesy of Wet Style, 71

David Whittaker, 108

II x IV Design Associates Inc., 32 (bottom left); 76

Paul Warchol/Resolution 4 Architecture, 88; 98 (right); 125 (left)

Stephen Wild Photography, 129 (right); 137 (left)

About the Author

Katherine Stone is a well-known interior designer and host of HGTV's *Lofty Ideas*. For more than 20 years, she's been designing residential and commercial interiors. She converted her first loft more than 15 years ago, when she turned an old warehouse into an open-concept office for her design firm, Stone & Associates. When she's not traveling to some of the world's greatest lofts, Katherine continues to design interiors and explore innovative design ideas. Katherine lives in Canada. Visit her Web site at: www.stone-and-associates.com

Acknowledgments

My eternal gratitude to the talented people who took the time and effort to contribute images of their outstanding designs and products. Special thanks to: my daughters Laura and Charlotte for their encouragement and editing skills; Patrick Blednick for his invaluable advice and for being so generous with his time; the ladies at Rockport Publishers—Betsy Gammons for her guidance and kindness, Kristy Mulkern for her patience, and Winnie Prentiss for enabling my vision to come to life; Jeffrey Solberg and Nelson French for jumping on my bandwagon with enthusiasm, energy, and promotional skills; and finally, Tim Alp, producer of *Lofty Ideas*, for sending me on the road to see the most amazing lofts in the world.